KU-580-703

Audio Programs

*33 Spirit Journeys**

Angels! Angels! Angels!

Cellular Regeneration

*Complete Relaxation**

Dreams

*Journeys into Past Lives**

Life Force

Past Lives and Beyond

Phoenix Rising

The Way of the Drum

Video

Instinctive Feng Shui for Creating Sacred Space

*Available from Hay House

Please visit:

Hay House UK: **www.hayhouse.co.uk**
Hay House USA: **www.hayhouse.com**®
Hay House Australia: **www.hayhouse.com.au**
Hay House South Africa: **www.hayhouse.co.za**
Hay House India: **www.hayhouse.co.in**

A Guide for Creating Your
Own Vision Quest

Denise Linn and Meadow Linn

HAY HOUSE

Australia • Canada • Hong Kong • India
South Africa • United Kingdom • United States

First published and distributed in the United Kingdom by:
Hay House UK Ltd, 292B Kensal Rd, London W10 5BE. Tel.: (0) 20 8962 1230;
Fax: (0) 20 8962 1239. www.hayhouse.co.uk

Published and distributed in the United States of America by:
Hay House, Inc., PO Box 5100, Carlsbad, CA 92018-5100. Tel.: (1) 760 431 7695 or
(800) 654 5126; Fax: (1) 760 431 6948 or (800) 650 5115. www.hayhouse.com

Published and distributed in Australia by:
Hay House Australia Ltd, 18/36 Ralph St, Alexandria NSW 2015.
Tel.: (61) 2 9669 4299; Fax: (61) 2 9669 4144. www.hayhouse.com.au

Published and distributed in the Republic of South Africa by:
Hay House SA (Pty), Ltd, PO Box 990, Witkoppen 2068.
Tel./Fax: (27) 11 467 8904. www.hayhouse.co.za

Published and distributed in India by:
Hay House Publishers India, Muskaan Complex, Plot No.3, B-2, Vasant Kunj,
New Delhi – 110 070. Tel.: (91) 11 4176 1620; Fax: (91) 11 4176 1630.
www.hayhouse.co.in

Distributed in Canada by:
Raincoast, 9050 Shaughnessy St, Vancouver, BC V6P 6E5. Tel.: (1) 604 323 7100;
Fax: (1) 604 323 2600

Cover design: Louis Zimmerman • *Interior design:* Nick C. Welch

Originally published in 1997 by Random House (ISBN: 978-0-7126-7292-4).

The information given in this book should not be treated as a substitute for professional medical advice; always consult a medical practitioner. Any use of information in this book is at the reader's discretion and risk. Neither the authors nor the publisher can be held responsible for any loss, claim or damage arising out of the use, or misuse, or the suggestions made or the failure to take medical advice.

A catalogue record for this book is available from the British Library.

ISBN 978-1-84850-894-1

Printed and bound in Great Britain by CPI Group (UK) Ltd, Croydon, CR0 4YY.

*I dedicate this book to my husband, David,
who makes my heart sing and my spirit
soar to the furthest horizons.*
— D.L.

*I dedicate this book to my friends, family,
and teachers who were part of my Quests
and taught me the value of solitude.*
— M.L.

CONTENTS

PREFACE

In ancient cultures throughout the world, Quests were used as doorways to enter spiritual realms. A Quest could take the form of a retreat into nature, a Vision Quest, or a pilgrimage. Through these extraordinary inner journeys, sacred visions revealed personal direction and life purpose. Traditionally, Western culture has had no equivalent rite of passage. We could only imagine how those ancestral people accessed the mystery and wonder that exist at the core of life. However, with the resurgence of interest in spiritual beliefs that are closely interrelated with nature, many people have yearned to return to their spiritual roots. They have felt the call of the Quest.

Over the years, people from 18 nations have come to the Vision Quest seminars that I have led in various locations around the world. The experience has been immensely rewarding and fulfilling. When participants arrive for a Quest, I hear the same heartfelt concerns time and again: "Who am I?"; "What is my purpose?"; "How can I live a life that matters?"; "What can I do to heal my relationships?"; "How can I get closer to Spirit?"; "How can I be happy?" Each person comes wanting to find a sacred space within that is real and honest and true.

As the Quest seekers retreat into nature in solitude, shifts of consciousness begin to occur. Old memories come to the surface to be resolved. Fear is confronted. A sense of purpose emerges. In the heightened state of awareness that a Quest elicits, archetypal images can appear. A tree becomes a sage. A cloud becomes an angel. A power song is received. A voice speaks out of the darkness. The unexplained and mysterious occur. Understanding of self deepens, and remarkable transformations often take place.

The magic of watching someone confront fears or take the first steps toward the accomplishment of lifelong dreams has been one of the most fulfilling aspects of my work. Letters received from participants years after their Quests have confirmed that the results are long lasting and far-reaching. It's the satisfaction I have gained from these observations that made me want to share the Vision Quest experience with a wider audience.

To gather anecdotes for this book, a written request was sent to a number of people who had participated in my Quests. The responses at first came in at a trickle, then rapidly turned into a deluge of letters from many different countries. I was amazed and delighted by both the number and the intensity of the responses I received.

Reading the letters was a very gratifying experience. A consistent theme was the lasting value and impact that the Quest has had on participants' lives over the years. Many of the glowing adjectives contained in the letters ("It was absolutely amazing"; "It changed my life forever"; "Absolutely the best thing that I have ever done") weren't used for the sake of journalistic balance because they were too effusive. I have not included some of the most remarkable stories because I thought they would stretch credibility; however, I personally know they are true. I also left out many of the most touching letters because of the personal nature of the comments, while I omitted others to avoid duplication of themes. Deciding which letters to include was a difficult task, as each clearly came from the heart.

A number of quotes refer to the island where I used to lead my Vision Quests. Quest participants stayed in tepees during the preparation time on the island, which was surrounded by seals, eagles, otters, and whales. Wild deer and raccoons roamed through the island's forest. Many of the remarks reflect the beauty of this special place. To protect the privacy of the island's owners, in this book I have changed the name of the island to Sacred Island. It's a fitting name because the island is considered a sacred place by the local Native Americans.

In crediting the sources of the experiences, some people asked me to use their full names, some asked that their names be changed, others wanted only their first names used, and some asked me to use the spiritual names that came to them on their Quests. I have honored these requests.

Meadow Marie Linn, my daughter and a veteran of six Quests, co-wrote this book and also wrote the chapter about Quests for teenagers when she was 18 years old. She included journal entries and parts of letters that were sent to her by her friends from the Mountain School in Vermont who shared a four-day Quest with her. Meadow and I both feel passionately about the value that can be garnered through a retreat into nature. We feel that by combining ancient wisdom and contemporary techniques, you can truly journey to the center of your soul.

CHAPTER ONE

In Quest of a Vision

*On the second night of my Quest, I stretched out and lay
back filled with the most indescribable peace. Staring up at
the night sky aglow with a trillion stars, I started to feel utterly minute with the cosmos stretched out above. Who is this
I? What purpose does it have in the whole scheme of things?
What was I about to find out about myself? What long-sought
answers to questions will I receive? Intoxicated by the imme-
diacy of nature and feeling as insignificant as a grain of sand,
I drifted effortlessly into a deep sleep. All I knew for sure was
that this Quest, whatever else it may be, felt absolutely right for
me in that moment.*

—Tessa Dace

There's a realm beyond the physical senses. It's a realm of
mystery and spirit. It's an infinite and eternal dimension that
transcends form and goes beyond time and space. The search for
this domain has gripped the hearts of human beings throughout
history. From the early biblical prophets who walked alone
into the desert to fast and pray for divine revelation to Native
Americans setting out into the wilderness to search for a vision,
the pursuit of an inner world, beyond everyday physical reality,
is one of humankind's oldest traditions. For thousands of years
humans have retreated into nature in solitude to find answers to
life's questions and to gain spiritual wisdom. Though many of the
old ways have been forgotten, there remains a means by which
anyone can step through the crack between two worlds and enter
mystical dimensions. This retreat, this Quest, is an ancient rite of
passage; it's a journey to the center of your soul.

As we hurtle into the future, the trappings of modern life isolate us from the earth and leave little room for the inward journey. We're losing the ability to listen to the stirrings of our soul. In our urban communities we've lost an immediate connection with nature, which is the most powerful purveyor of visions, signs, and messages from the realm of Spirit. We've forgotten how to look for these signs, how to listen to the messages in the winds, and how to gain wisdom from the trees. Earning money, keeping up with technological advances, and raising a family make it difficult to still the mind and open the heart. Hence, very few people truly understand what forces have motivated their life or have shaped their destiny.

Going on a Quest is a powerful way to reclaim a sense of wonder and connection to the earth. It can take the form of a journey into nature for solitude and for introspection that encourages answers to personal questions to rise from within. A process of simplification then occurs where you discover what is truly important in your life. You can begin to reach the source of any pain you may have so that it can be healed. A Quest can also give you certainty about your future, as well as help you develop spiritual depth. It's an act of power that can change your life forever.

There are many ways to embark upon a Quest in present times. You can trek into the wilderness where spiritual realizations are gained through survival or make a pilgrimage to a sacred site. However, a Quest can be as simple as taking an afternoon to sit in stillness in a forest or experiencing solitude indoors in a specially prepared room.

One form of Quest requires sitting in nature for three to four days and nights, calling for a vision that gives guidance about one's life. In ancient native cultures this tradition, called a Vision Quest, was often used as a rite of passage into adulthood because it was felt that the visions received by young men or women helped determine the roles they would play as adult members of their tribe. Later in life they would continue to use this ritualized retreat whenever they needed to gain help from the Spirit powers.

For those tribal people, the Vision Quest was an extension of a religious experience that was based on the earth they walked on, the sky above them, and the beauty of nature that permeated every waking moment. Life was seen as one long, mystical sojourn in which the Creator spoke to them through every sunrise and every evening breeze. They knew they were constantly surrounded with messages and signs from the spiritual realms, and the Vision Quest allowed them to be still long enough so that they could listen intently to these messages.

In ancient Native American tradition, a vision seeker usually climbed a mountain or went to a special place in nature. Sometimes their sacred site, or "dreaming place," was a pit dug into the side of a hill. Usually the seeker sat in the center of a special circle of stones (a medicine wheel) that created a safe and holy place. Often, this place for vision seeking had been used by the family for generations. The length of the Vision Quest varied from tribe to tribe; however, the seeker usually stayed for four days and nights without food (and in some traditions without water). A man named John Lame Deer, who later became a medicine man, describes his Vision Quest, near the turn of the 20th century, when he was a boy named Johnny Fire:

> Here I was, crouched in my vision pit, left alone by myself for the first time in my life. I was 16 then, still had my boy's name, and let me tell you, I was scared. I was shivering and not only from the cold. The nearest human being was many miles away and four days and nights is a long, long time. Of course when it was all over I would no longer be a boy, but a man. . . .
>
> Blackness was wrapped around me like a velvet cloth. It seemed to cut me off from the outside world, even from my own body. It made me listen to the voices within me. I thought of my forefathers who had crouched on this hill before me. . . . I thought that I could sense their presence. . . . Sounds came to me through the darkness: the cries of the wind, the whisper of the trees. . . . I felt feathers or a wing touching my back and head. . . . I heard a voice that was human. . . . A voice said, "You are sacrificing

yourself here to become a medicine man. In time you will be one." Slowly my fear left me . . . I felt power surge through me like a flood. . . . When old man Chest [his uncle] came for me, he told me I was no longer a boy. I was a man now. I was Lame Deer.[1]

A Quest of any kind is a heroic journey. It's a rite of passage that carries you to an inner place of silence and majesty and encourages you to live life more courageously and genuinely. The benefits of a Quest are numerous. A Quest can help you to:

- Discover who you are
- Connect more deeply to nature
- Define your life goals
- Find your purpose
- Gain power and clarity
- Connect to your higher self and the Creator
- Meet your guides, totems, and allies
- Find your true name
- Overcome fears and self-imposed limitations
- Heal abuse, grief, and anger issues
- Heal relationship issues

One of the most profound benefits of a Quest is the discovery of who you are through exploring the patterns in your life. There are consistent patterns in all things. These templates for life have grace, rhythm, and symmetry and are a part of the great web of the universe. You can find these patterns in the way branches circle a tree or the wind shifts desert sands, as well as in the changing of the seasons and in the continuous cycle of birth, death, and rebirth. They also exist within and throughout your life. In the stillness of a Quest you can examine your life's recurring cycles.

Wilma Hartmann, a communications consultant from South Africa, wrote to me about how her Vision Quest helped her to discover who she was and to realize the rhythms in her life:

During my Quest I sensed a great awareness of cycles. Cycles of day and night, of the sun, the moon, the sound of the tides, of the whale coming back every morning. I sensed my own rhythm. In one contradiction, things both slowed down and sped up. I was intensely aware of Great Spirit being the rhythmic heart pulsing inside me and in everything around me. Everything being one.

Looking back, my Vision Quest dreams leap at me. They are still extremely vivid. One upon the other, they were like skins of fear being peeled away. My dreams were filled with anxiety, fear of change, fear of being rejected, fear of exploring the unknown. Bit by bit I worked beyond the fear until I knew that the life I had was the one I wanted. It was no longer the boring life, forced upon me by responsibility and sense of duty.

I left the island with heightened perceptiveness, with inner strength and a feeling of being part of a great universe. My arms could reach far and wide. Like cool water being drawn through the center of a big strong tree. I came back home, unable to give words to what I had experienced.

Sometimes a Quest can act as a catalyst for old issues to surface and heal. Lisa, an advertising executive in Hong Kong, had a very powerful emotional experience that began a healing process for her regarding childhood sexual abuse issues:

I got really angry about not having any water for most of the second day. I had a leaky water bottle. I stormed off my little hump of grass and stamped back to the lodge thinking that I was going to let everyone know just how unfair this water business was. I ranted at an assistant and she burst into tears. Then I went in to attack you [Denise]. I hated you at that point.

You said at the time that the water incident must hold a learning experience for me, that my anger must have a root in the past. No surprise. Of course you were right. Usually, rather than express my emotions in the form of tears, I would cry inside myself. The result of this was that when I was emotional, I wouldn't cry, but I would urinate profusely. I realized that having no water had been set up at some level to bring me face-to-face with the water issue, or more accurately, with the natural expression of my emotions.

I had always been aware of my ability to leave my body in times of pain but did not understand the causes. Though I didn't know it at the time of the Vision Quest, the disconnection with my emotions was brought largely through early and forgotten sexual and emotional abuse. The Vision Quest was the stimulus for a period of exploration and discovery. It allowed me to come to terms with my emotional fragmentation and the integration of the different parts of me. The Vision Quest started a process by which I have worked through heaps of emotional stuff from my younger years . . . rapes and attempted rapes. As a result of this work, one year later I weighed 135 pounds (at the time of the Quest I was around 200 pounds). The insights and way of viewing the universe that I gained have become increasingly integrated into my daily life.

Many people find that a Vision Quest helps them to overcome fear. Julie Robertson told me how the Quest helped her confront fear. She had a difficult time finding the right spot for her Quest. "Suddenly I stumbled across a little clearing. It was about nine feet around, in a circle of trees, the perfect size for a medicine wheel." However, once she sat in her circle she began to feel afraid. As late afternoon shadows lengthened with the approach of evening, Julie began to feel even more frightened. She heard many inexplainable sounds in the surrounding woods that "froze" her "with terror." She told me that she was so scared she felt like she was in a "waking nightmare," but then, as she accepted her fear, she began to understand the deeper significance of her Quest; her fear was a catalyst for healing and forgiveness:

As I stared in tired misery at a clump of nearby trees, I felt I was hallucinating. Then the pattern of a mottled feather appeared in the trees. I closed my eyes, reopened them, and the feather was still there. Slowly the face of a tawny owl formed over it. I realized that this was a message from Great Spirit that the owl was my guide. At this point, I thought of everyone I'd wronged, apologized to them, and mentally hugged them. Then I thought of those who had wronged me, and I forgave them. Tears flowed as I experienced total forgiveness of my mother. The wind whispered through the trees, "You have done well," and then the trees all swayed gently above me, as if looking down and nodding in agreement. And so the process continues, which sprang from my Vision Quest. That was a time I shall remember forever.

Sometimes a Vision Quest can carry you into mystic and wondrous realms. This occurred for Krystel Nicol, a young woman with a gentle demeanor. She arrived for the Vision Quest without a clear direction but found that her Quest opened her to something precious and magic inside herself.

I didn't really know why I came to the Vision Quest, I just felt impelled. I spent most of the time on the island before the Quest trying to come to terms with just being <u>Me</u> . . . the negative Me, the jealous Me, the angry Me, the petty Me, the selfish Me . . . and the frightened Me. The first night of the Vision Quest as I lay down to go to sleep, I felt very frightened of the dark. . . . I was so scared that I even began to tremble as I lay in my sleeping bag. Then I began hearing the delicate sounds of bells ringing . . . followed by the soft muffled sound of a gong. I then heard voices coming closer. My fear receded when I heard the voices. As I strained to hear what they were saying, I was amazed to hear the voices whispering my name. As I listened more intently, the voices became more distinct. I heard them say, "Don't be afraid. You are safe. We are here watching over you." The next thing I remember it was morning, and deer were eating near the lake not far from my Vision Quest circle.

Later that day at sunset, I heard breaking sticks behind me. I slowly turned around to see a beautiful softly dappled doe standing on the moss-covered forest floor not far from my circle. She blinked. I closed my eyes and silently told her not to be afraid. When I opened them she was still standing and watching me. Very slowly, very calmly she walked closer. Hesitating for just a moment, she stepped into my circle and gently brought her face next to mine. I could smell her. I could feel her warm breath on my cheek. I looked directly into her eyes and she let me see her spirit, and I let her into my heart. For a second it felt like our spirits were one, and I knew her totally and she knew me. She showed me how to open my heart, she opened a pathway for the real Me to start to grow, and for the first time in my life I felt complete!

A Vision Quest can allow you to experience everyday life in a new and vibrant way. Janna Bristow, a dental technician, found in the silence of the night a power that enriched her day-to-day life:

On the second night I had quite a rough time. I had tapped into all sorts of shadow lands and found myself feeling immensely small and lonely, cold, and very hungry. I have never felt so exposed and so tremendously alone. Time stood still and the night seemed to stretch on forever. I was scared but couldn't understand what really frightened me. The darkness sought me out and exposed me. I sensed I was being watched, watched by the trees, the rocks, the sky, and all the creatures I could not see. The silence was excruciating.

I can imagine how some people feel they are losing their sanity when there's just no sound. As I lay there in darkness, unable to move or to distract my mind, I began to connect with the beauty of the silence. It makes me tearful just telling of it, I never want to lose it. Now I can be in the midst of everyday hectic life and I am able to tune in to my inner self, knowing that the great depth of silence is not lost. After a few hours, scenes of incredible beauty . . . mountains, rolling hills, lush green valleys, deep blue lakes, and powerful waterfalls filled my vision. I had entered an altered state of consciousness. It was incredibly soothing and comforting to be able to connect to the spirit world with such ease. I never thought it possible. I then fell asleep for a short while just before dawn.

Some people think that, on a Quest, one's purpose can be discovered only through struggle and strife. Although the recognition of purpose can come through sustained effort, it can also come as a gentle recognition that you *are* living your purpose, an awareness that everything you do and have done in your life is meant to be. However, until you have this realization, it seems that life is without purpose. But life isn't always a mystery to solve; perhaps it's more a reality to experience. Graham Walkinshaw, a crisis counselor from Scotland, talked about his Quest and his realization:

My Quest was not spectacular. I was hoping for some dramatic vision or visitation. I had positioned my medicine circle near to the shore, as I knew that orca whales swam in the waters around the island. Their presence was one of the reasons for my coming to the island to do the Quest. My scientific left-brained mentality, which I have always struggled with, wanted some physical encounter, like a message from an orca, to prove the existence of the visionary world. I suppose that I only partially acknowledged this to myself as I never really expected this kind of thing to happen to me.

In the end, I sat quietly in the same place for two days just being.

Thinking about this now, the simplicity of what I did is quite surprising. I sat on one part of the planet for a couple of days and . . . was! I spent a long time watching the ants. A sea otter leaped out of the water, scurried around in the undergrowth, then returned silently to the sea. A deer walked right past me, an arm's length away, eating the green grass and moving on without the slightest glance in my direction. Many birds came and went, seemingly oblivious to my existence as I just sat and watched.

It wasn't until I came to write this that I began to appreciate fully the lesson of quietly sitting in one place for a while. I am so used to the hurry and noise of the world that I had forgotten how it was to be simply sitting. I suppose my scientific left-brained self can't believe that the answer is so simple. Just be!

Visions can come in many ways, and calling for a vision can be a lifelong process. However, there's power in setting aside time in your life for a Quest. Your personal Quest should consist of six parts.

1. Purpose

This step entails defining the purpose of your retreat. What is your reason for going on a Quest? Is there an area of your life that needs healing? Do you need to step beyond fears that are immobilizing your life? Do you need to seek a new direction in life? Do you need some time just to be still, without having to do anything? These are all valid reasons to embark on a Quest. Where your intention goes, your energy flows; as you define the purpose of your Quest, the universe will propel you in the direction of your intention.

2. Preparation

What kind of Quest are you going to do? How long will your Quest be? What location have you chosen? Are you going to use a preparatory program? Have you dealt with all obligations and cleared the time for your Quest? All these questions should be addressed before you go on your Quest.

3. Leaving the World Behind

On a Vision Quest you leave the comfort of the boundaries of your environment and venture beyond what is safe and secure. When one is always in comfortable surroundings, decisions and experiences are often based on repetitive, preconditioned responses. These responses are determined by one's environment, friends, and family. When you take the risk of stepping out of the boundaries of your everyday experiences, a fresh new way of seeing yourself and the world around you can evolve. This can be done ideally by going into nature. However, as urban life consistently makes demands on our time and resources, a Quest can also occur in a sheltered environment where you do not need to do anything and there are no external distractions, such as the phone or visitors, so that you can truly "leave the world behind."

4. Life Evaluation

Who are you? What are you? Often we do things to give ourselves the impression that we exist: How do you know that you exist? What really gives meaning to your life? What are your priorities? Are you satisfied with your career and your relationships? Every act creates its own consequences. What are the consequences of your acts? Are you happy with the way your life is going? During this part of the Quest, you evaluate your personal history and face your fears and your death. This is the time to observe repetitive negative patterns in your life and to step beyond limiting definitions of self. This is the time to realize that you are *not* your past history, culture, society, religion, economic level, race, heritage, family, sex, body, or even your feelings and emotions. It's during this period that you explore who you truly are. When you take the time to examine your past, it prepares you for your future.

5. Being Open for a Vision

The next step is to let go and be completely open to Spirit. Quieting the mind is important because only when you're empty can you be filled. In the stillness you can "be" in present time, observe the signs in your surrounding environment, and listen to the whispers of the universe. This is the time of symbolic death and rebirth into a new way of being in the world. Learn how to live a life that matters. Your vision helps shape your destiny, and those who find their destiny find happiness.

6. Returning Home

Endings are as important as beginnings. Give yourself time to reenter your life slowly and to integrate your experiences. When you cross the threshold back into the ordinary world, you may feel reluctant to return. Overpowering reluctance may be a form of self-indulgence. You have taken a sacred inner journey, and now you're returning to your everyday life to give something of what you gained from your experience to each individual you meet and to the world at large. This is the power of the Quest.

If you decide to go on a Vision Quest, it's best to work with someone who has led these experiences before. However, in modern life it's not always possible to have a shaman or a guide as you seek your signs and visions. You can therefore create a modified Vision Quest for yourself. This book gives you the information that you need. Chief Crazy Horse said in 1850: "A very good vision is needed for life, and the man who has it must follow it—as the eagle seeks the deepest blue of the sky." It's important to take time off from your daily life in order to renew and restore yourself, to come into balance with all things. A Vision Quest may be the single most significant thing that you do in your life.

CHAPTER TWO

PREPARING FOR YOUR QUEST

Your Quest starts the moment you make the choice to go. This decision is a heroic step, a commitment to discover and embrace who you are. Your commitment is your word to the universe and to yourself that you will embark on this sacred journey, and there's power in that. Remarkably, once you have made the choice, it may seem as if life conspires to prepare you for your Quest. Sometimes old issues and personal blockages begin to surface for release during your retreat. Sometimes, opportunities present themselves, almost magically, to ease your inward journey.

"Forces will have been set in motion beyond the reckoning of the senses. Sequences of events from the corners of the world will draw gradually together, and miracles of coincidence will bring the inevitable to pass."

—JOSEPH CAMPBELL[1]

After making your commitment to go on a Quest, decide what kind you want to go on. There are many different sorts to suit your personality and lifestyle. You may decide to go on an organized, guided Vision Quest, go on your own or with friends, choose from a number of "alternative" Quests, or make a pilgrimage.

There are individuals and organizations that arrange Quests. Some are focused primarily on the Vision Quest, while others include a Vision Quest as only a part of their program. (See Further Information at the back of the book for more details.) If you prefer an organized Quest, it's very important to do some research into the program and its leaders. Some are aligned with Native American traditions, while others have more emphasis on personal development. Some are aimed at a particular topic, such as a Vision Quest for women to help overcome emotional blockages as a result of sexual abuse. Some Quests are designed to be physically strenuous, and some are less intense. There's no kind of Quest that's intrinsically better than any other; the best Quest is the one that's best for you.

Ask the organization to give you the names of some previous participants so you can talk to them about their experiences and their opinions of the leaders and organization. Don't be afraid to ask questions. The more confident you are about the program you choose, the better prepared you'll be for your Quest.

When looking for someone to be a teacher or guide for your Vision Quest, choose one who meets these criteria:

- Radiates compassion and kindness
- Has a good reputation
- Is flexible in teaching style
- Has a confident presence
- Knows how to listen
- Accepts mistakes in self and others
- Isn't afraid to show emotions
- Has a good sense of humor
- Laughs at him- or herself
- Makes everyone feel valuable
- Has a playful side
- Is direct and truthful
- Shows respect for the environment
- Includes members of any race or culture

It's important to be careful in choosing the one with whom you're going to do your Vision Quest. However, in a deeper sense, there are no wrong teachers. The teacher you feel drawn to, from a higher perspective, will be the best teacher for you at that time in your life. Some of my greatest growth has come from teachers who were not "perfect" people. When I was in my early 20s, I was drawn to a teacher who said he was very spiritual and claimed to know great truths. He said if I trained with him, I too might become spiritual. Because I was unwilling to take responsibility for my life, it was simpler to submit to his authority. When I realized that this person wasn't as honorable as he had portrayed himself, it was a valuable step in my development. In this way he *was* the perfect teacher for me at that time. If he had been impeccably humble and compassionate, I might still be looking to him for answers and might never have realized that the answers are inside me. I honor the gift of his teaching, for it gave me what I needed then.

Support-Group Quest

A support-group Quest is a retreat that you organize with other people. This has the advantage of offering a mutually supportive environment during your Quest. If you decide on this option, it's a good idea to have several planning meetings. Areas to discuss:

- Where will your Quest be held?
- What kind of transportation will be needed?
- What supplies should be taken?
- Are you going to do a preparatory program beforehand?
- What are your safety contingencies? For example, where are the closest hospitals and other emergency services to your Quest site?

When choosing an area in nature, pick a place where you're not likely to be disturbed by others. Make sure that family and friends know exactly where your group will be and what your timetable is. If you're in a national park or in a forest give the same information to the rangers so that in the event of a natural disaster, such as a flash flood, they'll know where to find you.

If your group Quest will be outdoors, plan to have at least one person serve as a guardian who doesn't do the Quest but who sets up a base camp and conducts safety checks twice a day. (In my Quests, I have approximately one guardian for every five or six people.) In addition to the individual supplies listed later in this chapter, the guardian should have a first-aid kit, extra blankets, a camping knife, extra water, food, extra dry clothing in case of bad weather, and a means of communication such as a cell phone or a CB radio. Guardians can eat and do normal outdoor activities as long as their primary focus is the safety and well-being of the Questers. They may also want to focus energy and love toward the individuals while they're on their Quest.

A prearranged signal, such as a colored flag raised at the Quest site, should be decided on so that if a Quester needs anything, it can be easily obtained. A note left by the flag can give all the necessary information to the guardian. When I check on Vision Quest sites, I usually get an *okay* hand signal from the participants. No words are spoken. Often people sleep for long periods of time on their Quest. If the guardian checks and the participant is sleeping, the guardian should continue to check periodically during the day. Usually the Quester is simply taking a long nap, but just in case he or she has fallen ill, it's a good idea to continue to check and to ask the person if everything is all right.

Be sure to take a whistle with you on your Quest. If you need immediate assistance, a loud blast will bring other Quest members and/or the guardian to your assistance at once. Respect the importance of other people's Quests, and do not disturb them for any reason other than an emergency. Before the Quest begins, sit in your Vision Quest site and blow the whistle to make sure that others can hear you.

At the completion, many groups celebrate with a meal and share their experiences.

Independent Quest

An independent Quest is done without a group. However, do not go into the wilderness for a solo Quest without a guardian. Taking someone with you can be a good experience for both people. I know a couple who went into the wilderness for a Quest. The husband put up a tent and made a campsite while his wife created her sacred circle for a three-day Quest. The husband, an artist, painted the mountain scenery for the duration of his wife's retreat. The wife said that although she couldn't see her husband's tent, she felt safe knowing that he was close. They both found the experience very rewarding.

Alternative Quests

Although the kind of Vision Quest that I discuss in this book is a three-day outdoor retreat, there are many different ways that you can Quest. An alternative Quest can be as simple as having a day of silence. It's important to remember that results occur outside of time and space. They can occur as a direct outcome of your intention. If your intention is to transform and heal your life, it will happen no matter what form of Quest you take.

Garden Quest

Some people cannot go into the wilderness for a Quest because of health concerns, time constraints, or safety issues. For these individuals, an excellent alternative is a garden. Though this may seem less majestic than a Quest in the wild, a retreat in your garden or that of a friend's can be as powerful and life transforming as one on a mountain peak. *When your heart is open and your intention is clear, your vision will come, no matter where you are.*

The preparation for this type of Quest is the same as if you were doing your retreat in the wilderness, and your sacred circle is created in the same way as described in Chapter 3. However, if your garden doesn't have stones or twigs to make a circle, you may need to gather some beforehand. The equipment you need is essentially the same as for a wilderness Quest, especially if you're doing an extended one. However, you will probably go indoors to use the toilet and to replenish your water supply. You may want to sleep outdoors in your circle, but if you have health or safety concerns, you can sleep inside. A garden Quest can last from a few hours to a few days.

Indoor Quest

At some of my Quests, several individuals have chosen to do an indoor Quest for various reasons. In all cases they reported remarkable experiences, which has led me to believe that indoor Quests can be very beneficial. There are advantages to being in nature for your Quest, but in the winter or in bad weather you may prefer to be inside. An indoor Quest offers a warm, sheltered environment without concerns about weather, temperature, poisonous insects, or wild animals. It can be profound and moving, particularly if you have taken the time to prepare yourself and your surroundings.

When preparing for an indoor Quest, it's important that the room you use become a sacred space. To do this, pick a room where there's as much natural lighting as possible, preferably one with a view of nature but that offers privacy from the outside world. Once you have chosen the room, clean it thoroughly. Wash the windows. Scrub the floors. Clean cobwebs from the ceiling. As you clean, hold the intention that you are creating a sacred place. Clear out as much of the clutter in the room as possible. The more you can clear out of the room, the better. Once the room is clean, you may want to work with the energy in the room by using Space Clearing techniques.[2] To cleanse the energy in the room, take a small amount of burning sage in a fireproof bowl and circle the room, using a feather to disperse the smoke to purify the energy. You may then want to use a sprayer filled with water and essential oil to mist the room lightly. A combination of lemon, lime, and orange essential oils can help lift the energy in the room.

When the room feels good to you, bring in objects that represent energy, strength, healing, and love. For example, you might want to put a beautiful flower in a vase in the room or a healthy, vibrant houseplant, or place a faceted crystal in the window to make rainbows in the room when the sun shines. You can create your sacred circle with stones or twigs that you have brought in from outdoors or use objects that have special meaning to you. For example, I know a young woman who used crystals, feathers, and polished stones to create her circle.

Make sure that you have cleared the time, turned off the phone, and notified people of your intention so that they won't worry about you or disturb your Quest. There's a wondrous power that occurs when you take time just to sit still in a room within your sacred circle.

Day of Silence

Being silent for a day can be a type of Quest. Simply not talking for 24 hours can allow the internal chatter to become still to the point where you can begin to hear the whisperings of your soul. It may seem a bit contrived at first, but taking a day of silence can turn energy inward. To have a silent day, let friends and family know what you're doing so that you have their support and cooperation. Turn off the phone. And, no matter how tempting, don't answer the door. Don't read your mail or check your e-mail or Facebook account. Don't watch television, go online, or listen to the radio or stereo. If you have animals, try not to chat with them. Be still. You can walk around inside your home. You can take a walk outdoors if you're fairly certain that you won't meet anyone who will want to talk to you. You can prepare food. Taking 24 hours to be silent can bring profound insights into yourself and your life. Even if you live alone and don't usually talk during the day, the commitment to be silent brings a special energy. Start your day of silence when you wake in the morning and hold it until you wake the next day.

If you live with other people and it's absolutely necessary to communicate, use notes. Take Susan, for example, who was married and had three children. She told me she wanted to do a Vision Quest but didn't see how it was possible with the responsibilities of her family life. I suggested that she have a silent day. She talked to her family and they agreed to be supportive; in fact, the kids were excited: "Mommy isn't going to talk all day?!" Although a few times the children forgot and addressed her, for the most part they were very supportive. A babysitter took the children to the park for most of the day, and her husband looked after the children in the late afternoon and evening.

Susan said it was one of the most delicious experiences of her life. She sat in her garden under a large apple tree, sipped fresh mint tea, and watched the clouds sailing by. Everything seemed to slow down until whenever she moved she felt as if she were moving through golden honey. She noticed the way the oak tree had been full of gnarls in its life and then straightened again. She said that when looking at the oak tree she felt that the "gnarls" in her life would eventually straighten up again. She stretched out on the grass and seemed to be aware of the roots of the plants and the oak tree beneath the surface. She felt an awareness of the myriad activity in the earth: insect activity and even that of microorganisms beneath the surface. It gave her a sense of the living spirit that surrounded their home even though they lived in the city. The day of silence rejuvenated her and connected her to her spiritual roots.

Pilgrimage

A pilgrimage is a type of Quest. Though the form is different from the traditional Vision Quest, often the outcome is the same. Whereas a Vision Quest allows you to seek answers to soul-searching questions through the inward journey, a pilgrimage allows you to discover your life's meaning through the outer journey. In some respects, a pilgrimage is a mobile Vision Quest. You can call for a vision on your pilgrimage, and visions and insights can be received in the same way as on a stationary Quest. A pilgrimage is not just a physical journey through time and space, it's a powerful metaphorical rite of passage that can touch you as deeply as a Vision Quest.

When deciding whether to go on a Vision Quest or a pilgrimage, it's valuable to assess your temperament and the reasons for your Quest. All individuals need to create and express their inner journey in accordance with their needs and temperament. If you're always on the move and every day is filled with activity and you consistently direct your energies outward, the stillness and serenity of a Vision Quest might have a balancing influence on your life. However, if your life feels stagnant and you tend to be introverted, the pilgrimage may be the best kind of Quest for you. Having to deal with new and challenging external situations can catapult you from safe inward landscapes and allow the power and majesty of outer landscapes to transform you at the deepest level.

Where to Go on Your Pilgrimage

The location you choose is very significant. Is there somewhere that you have always felt drawn to? Is there a special place that fills you with excitement and wonder every time you hear about it? Following are some of the types of locations that you might consider.

A Sacred Site

There are many places that are thought to be charged with spiritual power, such as Stonehenge, Machu Picchu, and Lourdes. Some are widely known and some are known only to a few seekers. There's a deep current of energy that illuminates these places, and a pilgrimage to any one of them can connect you to the sacred space within you.

The Location of an Early Childhood Event

A pilgrimage to the location of your childhood can help reclaim lost or abandoned parts of yourself. Sometimes, returning to the place of your birth or the place of early childhood memories brings a sense of coming home to yourself. A pilgrimage to the past can also help heal childhood wounds.

An Ancestor's or Relative's Grave or Ancestral Lands

Taking a pilgrimage to a relative's or ancestor's grave or to your ancestral lands can be redeeming. When you reclaim a connection with your family roots and your lineage, it can have a sustaining and strengthening effect on your life.

Reliving the Journey of Another

In 1693, the renowned poet Matsuo Basho embarked on an 800-mile journey on foot through Japan's remote mountain regions, writing poetry the entire way. The pilgrims who follow his pathway today feel that his clarity and spirit imbued the land and created an energy that can still be felt. When you follow in the footsteps of another, it's valuable to attempt to see and feel as they did.

Feeling Compelled Without a Particular End Goal

Sometimes your destination becomes compelling even when you don't have any conscious reason for going. If you feel a deep inner need to journey to a particular place, listen to your heart and trust that there's a higher wisdom motivating you. Sometimes the reason will become obvious and sometimes you will never know, but nevertheless, it's important to follow the stirrings of your heart.

Your pilgrimage doesn't have to take you to foreign lands across great seas. It can be as simple as journeying to a nearby place of power or beauty. The earth has numerous places of power. Your pilgrimage can be to the top of a nearby mountain, to an ancient grove of trees, or to a cliff overlooking a lake or a sea. It's not the length of time you spend or the location you choose, it's truly your intention that makes your pilgrimage viable and powerful.

The Steps of a Pilgrimage

The steps of a pilgrimage are similar to those of a Vision Quest. Both involve a journey that separates you from ordinary life. Both involve an encounter with the sacred and then a homecoming. Following are some important steps to consider on your pilgrimage.

1. Intention

The first step in designing your pilgrimage is to clarify your intention. Why do you want to go? What specific results do you want? Take time to clarify for yourself exactly what your purpose is. This is similar to the first step you take before a Vision Quest. When you clarify your purpose, then everything that occurs on your journey is laden with meaning and value, and every experience propels you toward your goal.

2. Preparation

The preparation is both physical and emotional. Take time to plan for your physical needs. For example, if you're driving, is your car in good repair? If you're walking, do you have the right kind of shoes, and do you need maps? If you're going overseas, is your passport in order? Whether your pilgrimage takes only a few hours in the afternoon or is a month-long sojourn, it's vital to be prepared. Take a journal and use it. The experiences that may seem mundane at the time may be meaningful upon later perusal.

3. Separation from Ordinary Life

Both on a Vision Quest and on a pilgrimage, you leave the comfort of the boundaries of your environment and venture beyond what is safe and secure. Be willing to take a risk and operate without knowing the exact outcome of every decision. When you're always in comfortable surroundings, your decisions and experiences are often based on repetitive, preconditioned responses dictated by your environment, friends, and family. When you take the risk of stepping out of the normal parameters of your everyday experiences, a fresh new way of seeing yourself and the world around you can evolve.

4. The Journey

You can walk or drive on your pilgrimage. You can spend a few hours or a few months. You can choose a route that is easy or one that is challenging. The amount of time you spend, your method of travel, and the difficulty of reaching your destination are not as important as the intensity of your devotion to your journey. Your decision to go on a pilgrimage should not be made lightly. Once your journey begins, every experience you have is valuable and significant to the ultimate outcome. A pilgrimage is an act of power.

5. The Destination

Calling a trip a pilgrimage doesn't necessarily make it one. When you reach your destination, it's essential to stay in touch with the meaning of your pilgrimage. Take time to embrace the energy undercurrents of the place. Be open and receptive to the messages that are waiting for you at your destination. You have embarked on a long and perhaps arduous journey to attain your goal. Ask yourself, *Why am I here? What messages are here for me?*

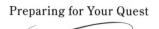

6. The Ceremony

In ancient times, pilgrimages were accompanied by ritual and ceremony. In present times, you can perform the rituals of the past or you can create your own. When you reach your destination, take time to honor your journey. From the simple act of placing a flower on a shrine, to creating a circle of stones, to offering a prayer, ritual actions affirm and deepen the meaning of your experiences.

7. Returning Home

Be as conscious at the completion of your pilgrimage as you are at its inception, for endings are as important as beginnings. Give yourself time to reenter your life slowly and to integrate your experience. When you cross the threshold back into the ordinary world, you may be reluctant to return. However, it's important to remember that you have taken a sacred journey, and now you are returning to give something from your experiences to each individual you meet.

Vision Walks

The American philosopher and poet Ralph Waldo Emerson wrote: "Every object, rightly seen, unlocks a new faculty of the soul." A simple alternative to making a pilgrimage Quest is to go out your front door with the intention that valuable insight will be gained during your walk. Then, watch for signs. This is especially powerful when you have a problem or challenge in your life. A Vision Walk can be a ten-minute walk or a long hike. Your focused intention and observation of signs sets this kind of walk apart from just an afternoon stroll.

Equipment for a Vision Quest

If you decide to go into the wilderness for your Quest, you will need to take equipment with you. Packing for this can help you clarify the form of your Quest through the decisions that you have to make. *Will I take this? Do I really need that?* This is not unlike the decisions you encounter in life. How much do you really want to carry in life? Realize that packing for your trek is an act of power. It's a transformative and empowering process. Do you really want to carry that much equipment? Are you denying your needs out of fear about what others will think? Your loaded backpack can be symbolic of your burdens in life. Notice how you feel about it after it's packed. Do you feel overburdened or perhaps incomplete? What do the different things that you've decided to bring say about you and your life?

Following are some items that you might consider bringing on your Quest. You may find that you don't need many of the things suggested. However, it's better to decide consciously beforehand what you want rather than be in the middle of your sacred circle and suddenly realize that with your fair skin, you should have brought a hat or sunscreen lotion.

Backpack

If you're hiking to your location, you might want to carry your equipment in a backpack. If you have never before walked with a backpack, load it up and practice wearing it ahead of time to see how it feels on your body.

Appropriate Clothing

Know the general climate of the area and pack enough clothing that you can layer for warmth or colder temperatures. If you're in cooler weather, bring a warm hat to prevent losing too much body heat. Remember that a climate that is comfortable when you're walking will feel substantially colder if you're just sitting and aren't eating. I have known minimalist individuals who have done their Quests nude, but this takes extreme discretion for reasons of personal privacy and changes in climate.

Waterproof Jacket

Even if the weather is fair, it's a good idea to have a jacket that can offer some protection from rain and wind.

Personal Items

What you decide to bring on your Quest is up to you. Some people prefer not to bring any personal items. However, others bring items such as a toothbrush and toothpaste, dental floss, a comb, hand cream, or feminine hygiene products.

Signal Flag

If you're doing a Quest with a guardian, it's valuable to have a signal flag to hang outside your circle to indicate that you need something. If you don't wish to speak, you can leave a note near the flag.

Sleeping Bag and Mat

Keep in mind the terrain as well as the climate when selecting your sleeping bag. I prefer the old-fashioned, oversized, cotton sleeping bags. They're made of natural fabric and don't make the rustling noise of the nylon or other synthetic sleeping bags. However, in a humid climate the cotton bags absorb moisture and are damp when you sleep in them. Cotton bags are also heavy to carry if you're walking far. Down sleeping bags are good for cold climates and are lightweight to carry. Fiber-filled bags are the best for rainy conditions. Some people like to bring a mat to place underneath their sleeping bag.

Pillow

If you choose to bring a pillow, a foam or polyfill is better than a feather one, as it dries quicker if it rains.

Groundsheets and Rain Tarps

It's a good idea to have a groundsheet to put under your sleeping bag and a tarp to put over you, in case of rain. The tarp should be about eight by ten feet. In addition, pack nylon cording in case you decide to tie up your tarp. A simple shelter can be constructed by tying a tarp by its metal grommets to nearby trees.

Flashlight

Bring a flashlight for emergencies. Check the batteries and make sure it's in good working order. A water-resistant flashlight is best.

Sunscreen and Hat

A hat and sunscreen are particularly important to prevent sunburn or sunstroke if you're going to be exposed to the sun.

Insect Repellant

Beware of taking so many precautions that you completely insulate yourself from nature. Insects are a part of nature. No matter where you have your Quest, unless you're indoors, there will be bugs. You can spend time groaning about what a nuisance they are, or you can realize that they're a vital part of Sprit's creation. If you decide to bring an insect repellent, try it beforehand to ensure that you're not allergic to it. Learn about the insects in the locale that you have chosen. If there are any poisonous ones in the area, check with local naturalists to find out the best strategy for dealing with them.

Journal and Pen or Pencil

For some, keeping a journal can deepen their experience. For others, the simpler the Quest, the better. If you decide to keep a journal, I suggest you start using it from the time that you decide to go on your quest. Also, consider how you want to keep your journal. Is it purely for you alone, or are you keeping it so that someday others (children, family, friends) can benefit from your experiences? Whom are you writing for? Your perceived audience can determine the form and style of your journal.

Toilet Paper and Small Trowel

Although some traditions maintain that you are not to leave the circle for any reason, most people prefer to go to the bathroom outside their circle. When you go to the bathroom, it's important that you do not harm the environment. Stay more than 200 feet from any water source. Also, for obvious reasons, bury your solid waste, using a small shovel or trowel.

Paper Bag

Used toilet paper should be put into a paper bag and burned at a later time. Alternatively, toilet paper can be put in a sealable plastic bag for a hike out. For environmental reasons, do not leave used toilet paper in nature, even if it's buried.

Large Water Container and Water

In some traditions, it's believed that a Vision Quest must be undertaken without water. However, I feel it's important that you have enough water on your Quest. The value gained from depriving your body of water does not equal the potential damage of dehydration. Please, drink plenty of water on your Quest. I suggest taking a gallon for each day that you are out. You do not need to suffer to grow spiritually. A plastic water container with a screw-on lid will serve the purpose. Sometimes, in the middle of the night, small animals will chew through water containers. If you are in an area with animals, reinforce the water bottles with insulating tape to prevent this. Do not drink any water from a natural source that has not been treated or filtered.

Food

Traditionally, Quests are done without food. Unless you need to eat for medical reasons (for example, if you are diabetic or hypoglycemic), you might try doing your Quest with very little or no food. As a culture, we tend to have many emotional issues surrounding food. Going without food for a few days can allow some of these issues to surface. However, there's no dishonor in eating during your Quest. If you do so, be very clear that it's your choice; do not feel guilty about it. Whether or not you eat doesn't determine the value you will gain. Rather, it's the way that you relate emotionally to the food issue that will determine the value gained. Whatever you choose to do, honor your choice and commitment. Personal power doesn't come from your decision about eating; it comes from making a commitment and abiding by it with no regrets.

Take food on your Quest that provides energy, such as fresh and dried fruit rather than candy bars and chips. Also, don't bring items that spoil easily without refrigeration. Nuts and dried meat are better sources of protein than are things that might spoil, such as tuna sandwiches. Take all the food for your Quest into your sacred circle with you. However, if you are in an area where animals may be attracted to your food, such as bear country, then the guardian may safeguard your food and bring it to you.

Duct Tape

Tape is an optional item, but if you're going to an isolated area, it can come in handy in numerous ways. For example, Dan rolled over his glasses in the middle of the night and broke them. He used duct tape to fix them. Duct tape can also close holes in sleeping bags or groundsheets and has a variety of other uses.

Checklist

- Clothing appropriate to climate and environment
- Waterproof jacket
- Personal items
- Sleeping bag and mat
- Pillow
- Groundsheet and rain tarp
- Flashlight
- Sunscreen and hat
- Insect repellant
- Journal and pen or pencil
- Toilet paper
- Paper bag
- Large water container
- Water
- Food (if needed)

- Duct tape

- Backpack

- Whistle

- Nylon cord

- Cell phone (for emergency use only)

Frequently Asked Questions

What exactly do I do on my Quest?

Sit. Stand. Lie down. Sleep. Think. Meditate. Stretch. Pray. Sing. Dance. Open your heart. Be still. Talk to God. Nap. Watch the environment around you. Breathe. Write in your journal. Cry. Laugh. Let go. Forgive. Heal. Love.

What if it rains? Should I stop?

If it rains, stake or tie up your rain tarp. However, rain during your Quest is an important part of your experience. Feel the rain. Become the rain. Listen to what it has to say to you. One of the most powerful Quests I ever conducted was in the rain. From the moment the Quest started, it rained. And then it rained harder . . . and harder. Some people ranted at the rain with anger and frustration. The rain became a perfect catalyst for unresolved areas in their lives. One person who was working through victim issues declared to the heavens, "Why are you doing this to me? Why me?" A person who had abandoned every major love relationship because she felt restricted said, "I want to leave. I feel so restricted in this damn rain."

Slowly, as one wet day slipped into another, a realization dawned for many. The rain wasn't a victimizer or a restriction or an angry god. The rain was just the rain. Afterward, I was told repeatedly by the Quest participants that the results were much more profound because of the rain. Everything that happens to you in your Quest can be a catalyst for change and growth.

What if I don't get any visions? Did I fail?

Some of the most profound, life-changing Vision Quests have been seemingly uneventful at the time. Meredith provides a good example of this. She said she felt she was just sitting in her circle. She watched the sun come up and watched it leave again. She felt peaceful at times and bored at times, but it seemed that nothing really happened. She had expected to see signs and have visions and amazing dreams. However, looking back, she reported that while on the surface nothing seemed to be occurring, something very profound was shifting inside her, because her life changed completely in the following year.

How long should my Vision Quest last?

If you're going on a Quest with a leader, usually the length of the Quest is predetermined. However, if you're going on a self-led Quest, I suggest you start with a very short time; even a few hours in stillness alone in nature can be valuable. You should work up to a longer Quest rather than jump right in. Remember, what's important isn't the amount of time you spend but the value you get from the time.

I've decided to do my Quest without food. How can I prepare for this?

Food can play a powerful role in our emotions, and often decisions and judgments about ourselves and our lives are based on food issues. Food can represent love; it can represent self-sabotage; it can also be associated with control issues. Eating is one of the most strenuous routines in life, and routines often can limit our spiritual growth. When you change your eating patterns, it can affect other habits, routines, and patterns in a positive way.

As your Quest looms ahead, notice any issues that arise around food. If you're clear that you're going to Quest without food, you might want to practice first. Try skipping a meal or two. Notice how you feel emotionally as well as physically. I recommend that you begin to change your eating habits during the week before your Quest. Allow your body to begin to detoxify. Cut down on fried and/or processed foods, meats, dairy products, and anything hard to digest. Eliminate alcohol and drugs (with the exception of prescription drugs). Increase your intake of fresh fruits, vegetables, brown rice, and fish. Cut down on caffeine, drink lots of water, and get plenty of sleep. In general, prepare your body to be as healthy and strong as it can be during your Quest. This preparation stage will increase your focus and readiness for your Quest.

Should I take my cell phone?

If you take your cell phone, use it only for an emergency. Ignore it otherwise. However, leave all your other electronic devices at home, such as radios, CD and MP3 players, and portable computers.

What about wild animals?

Animals can be a wonderful source of inspiration on a Quest. Some of the most magical experiences on Vision Quests have involved animals.

If you're going on a guided Quest, make sure that the leader knows about the animals in the area and gives you adequate information on any precautions that are needed. If you're going on your own, make sure that you and your guardian are well aware of any such precautions. For example, if you're going to an area where there are snakes, don't set up your site next to a snake habitat. Most animals in nature will not attack if unprovoked, but it's always best to be knowledgeable about the wildlife nearby.

Sophia attended one of my Quests. In the middle of the night she felt a rather large animal walk onto her abdomen. She lay very still as the animal proceeded to turn in a circle to make itself comfortable. It then curled up in a ball and promptly fell asleep. Sophia and the other Questers had been informed about the animals in our area, so she realized that the nestled body was a raccoon, which, though they can bite, are not usually dangerous. She said it was quite a wondrous experience having a wild animal sleeping on her all night. Sophia's experience with her furry visitor was a powerful, positive one because she had useful information about the animal and knew that her life was not in danger. For safety purposes, it's important to learn as much as you can about the local wildlife. It's also helpful in deepening your connection with the surrounding environment.

Can I leave my circle to go to the bathroom?

It's all right to leave your circle. Remember to be environmentally prudent with your used toilet paper.

What about washing myself?

Usually you don't wash; however, if not washing will distract you from your Quest, consider bringing a damp washcloth in a sealable plastic bag or disposable wipes. Some people feel the need to take a toothbrush and toothpaste. If you do this, please take care not to leave used toothpaste in the environment. Either bury it or, preferably, take it with you when you leave.

What if I feel ill? Should I stop?

If you don't feel well, tune in to your intuition to see what the best course of action is. If you feel that you are getting sick, have it attended to right away. Don't ignore the physical signals that your body sends you. However, sometimes you won't feel well because old issues are coming to the surface to be resolved. If this is the case, it's valuable to push through them. Sally felt a cold coming on during her Vision Quest. Her nose became stuffed up and her eyes began to water. Thinking that the cold was related to some underlying emotional issue, she meditated to examine her innermost feelings. Spontaneously, she began to remember long-forgotten incidents from her childhood. A well of grief filled her as she cried for the first time in many years. She felt that the cold was an important catalyst for her to resolve childhood traumas during her Quest.

If you are feeling ill and are the kind of person who toughs out the hard situations in life, please be aware that you do *not* need to tough it out. Sometimes the true act of power is to be willing to surrender and be easy on yourself. Suffering doesn't always build character; sometimes it's just suffering.

I have a medical condition. Can I go on a Vision Quest?

Anyone can go on a Vision Quest provided that the Quest is tailored to the individual's specific needs. If you have a medical condition, explain very clearly to your physician the nature of your proposed Quest. It's important that you have the approval and support of your doctor. If you're going on a guided Quest, make sure that the leader knows the exact nature of your condition and has the phone number of your health-care provider. In addition, make sure that someone checks on you periodically during each day. If for any reason you feel unwell, you must take care to guard your health, even if this means shortening your Quest.

There's more personal power gained by knowing what your body needs and making decisions based on that than by suffering needlessly. If you are doing a Quest without a leader, it's essential that, in addition to your physician's approval, you have a guardian who is within voice distance, can check on you during the day, and has your doctor's phone number. Provided that you approach your Quest with forethought and keep safety in mind, there's no reason why you can't have a successful Quest.

Should I continue taking my medication?

Absolutely. Under no circumstances should you stop taking any vital medication. You do not need to suffer to grow.

I'm diabetic. Can I go without food on my Quest?

No. If you are diabetic (or hypoglycemic or have any condition for which you must maintain a consistent calorie intake), it's *essential* that you bring along the food your body requires. In addition, make sure that you have the support of your physician.

What if I get scared?

One of the purposes of the Vision Quest is to begin to overcome fear. If a fear comes up, you can use your circle as a safe place to explore and release the fear. However, if you have a paralyzing fear, take steps to safeguard yourself emotionally. For example, if you are terrified of the dark, bring a flashlight with extra batteries. You may decide not to use it, but knowing that you have it can prove comforting.

Lena was utterly terrified of the dark. She always slept with the light on; she had never once slept in the dark. For Lena, the most terrifying thing in the world was to be alone in the dark. This fear paralyzed her. We discussed different options before her Quest. She had a flashlight to use, which eased her fear, and I told her I would continually check on her during the first night. We also talked about guardian angels and how she had an angel that looked over her during the night and day. After it got dark I went to check on her. I was amazed to find her relaxed and smiling—*and sitting in the dark.* This was a very dramatic switch from the white-knuckled terror she had experienced prior to beginning her Quest. She said, "My angel is with me. I feel so safe and protected. I am safe in the dark. I don't need you to come and check on me." Tuning in to her spiritual protectors, Lena had activated a sense of safety so that she was able to overcome her lifelong fear. She is no longer afraid of the dark.

Following is an exercise you can do if you become frightened on your Quest:

1. *Locate the exact place in your body where you are experiencing the fear.* Every emotion has a corresponding physical sensation and location in your body.

2. *Focus your awareness on that part of your body. Really feel the fear.* Usually when we experience fear, we do everything not to feel it. What you resist persists, so the harder you try not to feel fear, the more it will persist.

3. *Expand the sensation of fear and make it more intense.* Now, this might sound crazy. Why would anyone who was feeling afraid want to feel more fear? Two things occur when you do this.

First, when you are afraid, usually you are a victim of your circumstances and do not feel in control. When you choose to feel your fear rather than be the victim of it, you're in control. When you're in control of your fear, it will dissipate. Sometimes we pay money to be frightened. For example, we pay to go on a roller coaster or to a scary movie. The difference lies in the fact that you have consciously chosen to be afraid, so your fear does not become overwhelming.

Second, when you intensify your fear, you can uncover the experiences from the past and inner issues that continue to create that emotion. When you continually suppress your fear, you never have the opportunity to examine and deal with the underlying issues.

4. *Ask yourself the following questions:* If your fear had a shape, what shape would it be? If it had a color, what color would it be? If it had texture and temperature, what would they be? If there was a mood or a feeling (irritability, loneliness, melancholy, anger, sadness) associated with your fear, what would it be? Ask yourself these questions over and over as you continue to focus your awareness on your fear. Do this until you are the observer of your fear rather than the victim of it.

5. *Notice whether you have any memories associated with your fear.* If a fearful memory comes into your awareness, imagine that you're floating above it and viewing it from a higher perspective. Understand that every experience you have allows you to become a more integrated, compassionate human being—even experiences that you deem negative at the time. Once you have found a memory associated with the fear, see if there's an earlier similar memory. Keep going back through early memories until you find a "seed" memory so you can resolve it.

A seed memory is an original experience on which all future similar experiences are based. For example, if a dog bit a five-year-old boy, it might precipitate a future fear of dogs. Then, perhaps, when that boy was seven and riding his bike, a dog chased him. Having a fear of dogs, he might have become frightened and fallen off his bike. This experience would have strengthened and magnified his fear of dogs. Perhaps another time a dog barked at him, and he was so startled that he tripped and fell. Every experience magnifies (and subconsciously justifies) the original fear. Every similar experience is stacked on top of the original experience. To release a fear, going through the stack of fear experiences, one at a time, can help you get to the original experience. When you understand why the fear originated in the first place, often you can heal it. Many people have healed lifelong fears in the sanctity of a Vision Quest.

Another way of dealing with fear is to call on your guides, totems, and spirit guardians for assistance. This often proves to be a very effective way of dealing with fear (see Chapter 5).

Is there anything I can do to prepare for my Quest?

You might consider going through a preparation period immediately prior to your Quest. Although it's not essential, a process of physical and emotional preparation can have great value. You will have a much more powerful Quest if you have cleared space in your life beforehand. If you're thinking about the bills that need to be paid or the phone calls that you haven't returned, it makes it more difficult to focus on your Quest. In a deeper sense, when you clear space in your life you are symbolically clearing space within yourself. This can contribute to a more profound Vision Quest. There's power in symbolic acts. For example, if you clear clutter from your home, this symbolically contributes to clearing clutter out of your energy field. I recommend a 28-day preparation program (one full moon cycle) that is based on the medicine wheel. In this program, each week is dedicated to one of the four elements: air, water, fire, and earth. Each of these represents one of the four quadrants of the medicine wheel and each relates to a different aspect of your life: mental, emotional, spiritual, and physical.

You can initiate this program anytime throughout the year. However, when you begin, be aware of the cycle of the moon. It's ideal to start three to five days before the full moon or the new moon. This way, when you complete the preparation period, one month later, you will be Questing during either of these phases. The moon affects the energy of your Quest, so the phase of the moon during your Vision Quest is important. If you want to take some risks and dramatically change the course of your life, consider doing your Quest during the full moon, which is the time of activity and outer expression. If you feel the need to withdraw into yourself and awaken inner dreams and wisdom, consider doing your Quest during the dark of the new moon, which is the time of introspection and inner awakening. It's best to embark on your Quest immediately after the 28-day program.

The 28-day program can be done on your own or you can form a support group and do the exercises together, meeting once a week to give one another support. In the weekly meeting you can compare notes on personal progress and offer advice, assistance, and encouragement. During the meetings, a Quest location can be chosen, usually one where all participants can go together so that, for mutual support, they can be in close proximity during the Quest. (For an in-depth preparation for your Quest, please consider embarking on my 28-day Soul Coaching® program as detailed in my book *Soul Coaching*.)

Days 1–7
Air: Your Mental Self

This week is dedicated to clearing the mental self.

Deep within each of us are different aspects of our personality. The mental component is the part that discerns, analyzes, evaluates, and judges. The first seven days are devoted to clearing as many as possible of the cobwebs and unresolved issues that block the mental aspect of self so that you're mentally prepared for your Quest. Air traditionally represents the mental body, so this is also the time to be aware of the air around you and within you. Take a deep breath and be aware of the physical air around you. Concentrate on the air as it enters your lungs when you inhale and leaves when you exhale. Continue to do this periodically throughout each day of the entire week. By doing this you are activating the Sprit of Air that dwells within and around you.

During Air Week:

- Do things you've been putting off or make a plan to do them.

- Organize papers.

- Answer letters.

- Make postponed calls.

- Pay bills or make a schedule to do so.

- Organize your house and office space.

- Clear out the clutter in your home (if you don't love it or use it, get rid of it).

Days 8–14
Water: Your Emotional Self

This week is dedicated to clearing the emotional self.

The emotional aspect of self concerns intuition, trust, feelings, childhood emotions, innocence, and nurturance; and water traditionally represents emotions as well as purification and cleansing. Don't be concerned if emotional issues occur in your life during this week. All is not always as it seems. The issues that occur during this week can spur an awakening of deeper inner issues. This is part of a healing process.

For seven days, when you first awake in the morning, focus on the water around you and within you. According to some estimates, the human body is three-quarters water. In addition, there's always water in the atmosphere around you. Even in the driest climate there's always some moisture in the air. When you take a bath or shower, be aware of the cleansing and purifying aspect of water. Focus your awareness and attention on the Spirit of Water and continue to do this periodically throughout each day of the entire week. By doing this you are activating the Spirit of Water that dwells within you and around you.

During Water Week:

- Completely clean your house.
- Clean your office.
- Clean your car.
- Spend time evaluating your relationships.
- If you've wanted to say something to someone, now is the time to say it.
- Explore your dreams.
- Follow your intuition.

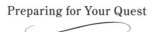

Days 15–21
Fire: Your Spiritual Self

This week is dedicated to clearing the spiritual self.

Fire is related to the spiritual aspect of self. It's your life force, the spark of life within you, the kundalini energy, the pure white light within, and the holy flame. Fire also represents transformation and change. Any spiritual blockages in your life may come to the surface during this week. This is the week to begin to change the old, limiting patterns and habits that can lock you into repeating negative cycles in your life. We often react to situations because of preconceived responses based on outmoded ideas about ourselves. Even tiny changes in your routine, such as changing what you have for breakfast, can help you begin to transform your definition of self. Don't be surprised if unexpected events or spiritual insights occur during this week. No matter what form they take, they will contribute to an expanded energy within yourself.

Each morning of the week, when you first awake, focus on the fire around you and within you. Light is an aspect of fire. If there's any sunlight in your bedroom, imagine that you are breathing in its light and power. Focus your awareness on the interplay of light and shadows in your surroundings. Fire dwells within you as your life force; it's the bioelectrical current that surges through the energy meridians in your body. Be aware of the inner flame within you. Continue to focus on fire in all its aspects periodically throughout each day of the entire week. By doing this you are activating the Spirit of Fire that dwells within you and around you.

During Fire Week:

- Meditate for 24 minutes a day on your inner light.
- Change your routines and your habits.
- Change your hairstyle.
- Take a new route to work.

- Try a food you have never had before.

- Buy that new outfit you thought was just a bit too wild (or elegant or casual) for you.

- Make a list of five things that get you all "fired up"—either angry or inspired—and take constructive action.

Days 22–28
Earth: Your Physical Self

This week is dedicated to clearing the physical self.

All the solid forms around you, including your body, are a part of the physical realm. Ancient peoples understood that everything we see and touch—every stone, every tree, our bodies, and the bodies of all creatures we encounter—are connected to the body of Mother Earth. This week is focused on your connection to physical reality. Be aware of the sense of grounding that your relationship to physical objects can give you. You're not separate from the universe. You're related to everything you see, touch, taste, hear, and encounter.

Every morning for seven days, when you first awake, focus on your physical environment. Be aware of the shapes and textures of the objects around you. Get a sense of the solid physical nature of your body. Notice how you relate and identify with the physical universe around you. Fully explore all the information brought to you through your bodily senses. Be aware of your time on this planet in the physical realm. Continue to do so periodically throughout each day during this last week. By doing this you are activating the Spirit of Earth that dwells within you and around you.

During Earth Week:

- Notice your relationship to all the physical objects in your home and life. What do they symbolize for you?

- Go for a walk every day. Spend at least 20 minutes in nature and silence.

- Attend to your health; for example, have your medical checkup, dental checkup, and so on.

- Get a massage or do something to contribute to your physical well-being.

- Go on a cleansing diet. Eat fresh fruit and vegetables; cut back on protein and animal products; drink lots of fluids.

Day 29: Preparation/Travel

Days 30–33: Vision Quest

CHAPTER THREE

THE SACRED CIRCLE

Your entire Vision Quest is a rite of passage and a ritual. Ceremonies are important in all cultures, past and present. Though they're more often associated with native cultures, rituals are still honored in Western cultures in rites of passage such as baptisms, marriages, graduations, and funerals. They mark the important transitions in life and offer a sense of continuity and security. In a deeper sense, rituals offer a way to express spiritual realities; they are physical enactments of inner spiritual voyages. They can allow for a deeper connection between the human and the divine realms.

One method of the Vision Quest entails using ritual and ceremony to create a circle out of stones or twigs within which to sit during your retreat. As you dwell within this sacred space, you participate in an ancient ceremony that spans generations and cultures. You then become part of a lineage that stretches behind you and unfolds in front of you. When you create your sacred circle, you are not only empowering the old ways but creating an energy for those who follow after you.

In past times, native people honored the sacred circle and what it represented. The circle was so important that it played a central theme in ceremonies throughout the world. Rituals of purification were performed in circular sweat lodges. When the elders came together in council, it was in a circle so that all were included, each having an equal say. Sacred dancing was performed in a circle. The circle evoked the feeling of completeness and wholeness; it allowed one to align with the center of the universe. The circle represented totality—the beginning and the end.

Although the use of a sacred circle during a Quest is universal, I have chosen to use the Native American term *medicine wheel* for the circle you will create on your Quest. To comprehend the medicine wheel, you must first understand the Native American concept of medicine, which is very different from traditional Western medicine. Native American medicine encompasses nature and concerns those things that help you to achieve a greater connection to Spirit. It increases your strength, health, and personal power and teaches you how to become more in balance with the world around you.

Your Vision Quest medicine wheel is a physical representation of the sacred circle that encompasses all life. It's an outer manifestation of an inner force. In its deepest sense, the medicine wheel is the pulsating cycle of energy that infuses all matter, animate and inanimate. It's symbolic of the mandala of the universe in which everything created has its appropriate place. It represents life, death, and rebirth. It contains the four elements and the four directions.

When you enter the medicine wheel on your Quest, you are stepping into a place of prayer. The center of the medicine wheel is sacred ground; it's a place of peace, calmness, and light. It represents a safe place where the Creator dwells. The Hopi Indians use the word *tuwanasaapi,* which means the place of belonging, the place where you're in your true home, the centering place, or the spiritual axis of the universe. The medicine wheel that you create for your Vision Quest becomes a point where you can pass between the visible and invisible realms. It becomes your centering place, your *tuwanasaapi.* It's a sacred place of openness, love, unmasking of the true self, sincerity of heart, transformation, giving thanks, and reaching a deeper connection with Spirit.

The medicine wheel is not only a sacred place for your Vision Quest, it's also a circle of protection. In ancient European tradition, the magi put circular shields around themselves that sealed them off from their surroundings. This circle of power protected them and became a place where energy could build. Those early mystics understood the sanctity of the sacred circle. Using ceremony, intent, and love, your medicine wheel can be a protected sanctuary where a vortex of spinning energy can build. As the vortex spins, your prayers can ride on this powerful energy and whirl up to your higher self and to God. This mystical, twirling energy of light and sound can take off the old and outdated parts of the self, while the seed of love inside you is purified.

The Wisdom of the Four Elements and the Four Directions

It's important to comprehend the significance of the medicine wheel that you create for your Quest. Your understanding will empower you. My perception of the sacred circle came from training with many native teachers. In most traditions the wheel is divided into four quadrants. Each of these quadrants represents different qualities, such as the four cardinal directions (East, South, West, and North) and the different elements (Air, Water, Fire, and Earth). Though the meanings vary among tribes and cultures, there's a general consensus concerning the power and value of the medicine wheel. Each cultural group has its own system for assigning various qualities, colors, elements, and totem animals to the cardinal points of the medicine wheel, and these vary widely among the traditions. In my search for understanding, I found this disheartening because I was searching for the "true" medicine wheel.

For several years I searched for the "right" wheel system. Then one day I realized that if one system was "right," the other systems were wrong . . . and this didn't feel good to me. *All* medicine wheel traditions have truth and beauty. The value of the medicine wheel is in the general way that it gives structure to the understanding and honoring of the cycles within us.

When I realized that the "true" medicine wheel was the one that was true to me, I decided to embark on a deep inner journey to find my wheel. Before I began my inward voyage, I prayed to the Creator and asked for a vision to show me what was best for me. My eyes closed; my breathing became deeper and slower. The raucous chirping of the birds at first seemed very loud, then faded to faint sounds until I was completely shrouded in dark silence. A deep sense of quietness came over me as the following images filled my mind and being:

Suddenly the darkness was pierced by a pinpoint of intense light. I felt myself being sucked toward that light. As I passed through a vortexlike portal of light, I felt alternate warm and cool shudders surge through me. Below me I saw a circular clearing in a meadow surrounded by mists.

As I floated down, I noticed that the meadow was surrounded by tall old trees. I intuitively knew that these tall silent guardians were each radiating loving wisdom and strength, creating a circle of power by their presence. Below me was a large circle of stones. Each stone was smooth and round, like a river stone smoothed by years of swiftly flowing waters; each seemed to shimmer softly in its own light. As my feet touched the ground, in the center of the circle, I felt intense freedom, power, and love emanating from the earth. A mist began to form around the circle.

I took a moment to be still. I then faced East and said, "Spirit of the East, help me understand my way in the world," and I stepped out of the stone circle into the mists. A soft wind began to swirl around me, shifting and changing. The light breeze became a whirling wind. I felt all the forms of air spiraling around and even through me. Cyclones, jet streams, zephyrs, tornadoes, and finally the stillness of a calm. Then, like a whisper, a delicate shimmer of energy rippled through the air as the wings of an eagle soared overhead. I felt the Spirit of Air "talking" to me. I gained the understanding that the element of air represents the intellect, mental clarity, focus, creativity, and inspiration. Taking a breath, I felt the Spirit of Air fill me. I realized that I was not separate from air, as it dwells within and around me. Giving thanks to the Spirit of the East, I stepped back into the circle of stones.

Facing South, I again stepped out of the circle into the mists. "Spirit of the South, hear me. Show me my way." Through the mists I saw overlapping images of gentle rains, waterfalls, mountain streams, gently undulating seas, fierce ocean waves, torrential rains, soft mists and fog, snow, and ice—all forms of the Spirit of Water. The Water Spirit spoke to me of emotions and childhood innocence and sacred dreams. I felt the water that flowed through my veins connect me to my feelings, to my childlike wonder, and to trust, and humility. I realized that I wasn't separate from the water that flows through and around me. Giving thanks to the Spirit of the South, I stepped back into the circle of stones.

I turned to the West and again stepped into the mists, calling for the Spirit of the West. Blazing, bright light illuminated the mists. Images of fire, from candlelight, to campfires, to forest fires, to the setting sun, filled my consciousness. The Spirit of Fire spoke to me of transformation and spiritual renewal. I was told that fire represents the alchemy that occurs when you release the old and embrace the new, as form changes and is transformed through fire. Fire changes old patterns and old habits; it's purification and renewal. The spark of life in every cell in my body is symbolized by fire. I recognized that I was not separate from the infinite sun and the life force within all things. Giving thanks to the Spirit of the West, I stepped into the circle again.

I faced North. Even before I entered into the mists, I felt the cold chill from the realm of the North fill me. As I stepped forward I experienced the immense power of the earth beneath my feet. Her many forms appeared and disappeared in the mists: her mountains, valleys, rolling hills, deep canyons, and vast plains. The Spirit of the Earth spoke of the physical realm of the world and the ancient wisdom that dwells in her depths. She spoke of balance, consolidation, and introspection.

With reverence I thanked the Spirit of the North and stepped back into the center of the wheel. The center is the point beyond the four directions and the four elements. It is the resting place of the Creator. It's the formless form, the place where beginnings

and endings merge. In the center I felt a deep sense of tranquil-
lity. I found my medicine wheel and was at peace.

As I listened to the whispers of Spirit in the four directions, I began to understand the cycles within my life, my own journey around the medicine wheel of life. I recognized that each part of the wheel symbolized a different aspect of myself and my life. Additionally, each quadrant of the medicine wheel represented a different aspect of my personality: the mental, emotional, physical, and spiritual aspects of my life. The beauty of the wheel philosophy is that the center of the circle is the place where all these aspects come together and are integrated; where all the parts of the self are in harmony. The center of the circle is the dwelling place of the Creator, where the forces of the universe merge into one.

My inner journey allowed me to comprehend the nature of the sacred circle. In further explorations, I discovered cycles within cycles of the medicine wheel. There's no end. The capacity for human development through the wheel is infinite. The sacred circle turns forever, and the journey never ends. It's a healing tool that can be used to soothe the soul by aligning with the elements and molding together the fragmented parts of the self.

My wheel of life gives me joy and stability. I have included the information I gained as a starting point to help you understand the power and beauty of the sacred wheel that you will create during your Quest. You may find that these meanings work for you, or you may want to discover your own personal medicine wheel.

The Spirit of the East

Symbolically, the beginning of the medicine wheel is in the East. The East is the home of new beginnings. It's the home of the spring, the dawning of the day, and the waxing of the new moon. New life. New birth. Seeds are planted. New sprouts push through the soil. Eggs in nests wait to hatch. Babies are born. The colors associated with the East are yellow and yellow-green, because this is the color of plants when they first sprout in the spring, filled with a potent life source. The element associated with the East is air, which symbolizes the mental aspects of the self. The key word is *inspiration*. The animal spirit keepers are the eagle, representing the masculine aspect of the East, and the owl, which represents the feminine. The eagle's realm is the day, which symbolizes the outgoing, projecting, yang forces of the universe. The owl's realm is the night, which symbolizes the inward, receptive, yin forces. In the creativity cycle, the East is the place of activation of ideas.

The Sprit of the South

Moving around the sacred circle in a clockwise direction, from the East you journey to the South. The South is the home of summer, the midday sun, and the full moon. Corn is high. Days are warm. It's the time of fullness and expansion. As the East represents the time of birth, so the South is associated with growth and the time of childhood. The element associated with the South is water, which symbolizes the emotional aspects of the self.

The color of the South is blue, for it symbolizes the deep blue of the sea and great waters. The animal spirit keepers are the frog and the dolphin, the masculine and feminine aspects of the South. The frog waits patiently for his prey and then projects his tongue with focus and precision. This represents the yang, masculine energy of linear projection and direction. The dolphin has a panoramic awareness of her environment, which is more yin, embodying the female principle of the universe. The key word of the South is *intuition*. In the creativity cycle, the South is the place where you nurture ideas.

The Spirit of the West

In the cycle of life, the West is the realm of autumn, the setting sun, and the weaning moon. Crops are harvested. Leaves are falling from the trees. In the human cycle, the West is associated with teenage and young-adult years, as these are the years

of change and maturation, discovery, transformation, and experi-
mentation. Fire is the element associated with the West, representing the spiritual aspect of life. The key word for the West is
transformation. The color associated with the West is the bright red
of the setting sun.

The animal spirit keepers of the West are the phoenix and the
snake. The phoenix (which can be likened to the thunderbird of
the Native Americans) is the masculine aspect, which embodies
the transforming nature of fire. The snake, the feminine aspect,
also represents transformation, as it changes when its skin is
shed. The snake (or lizard in some native cultures) is the keeper
of the dreamtime. In Hindu philosophy, the snake represents the
kundalini life force fire that dwells at the base of the spine and
has the power to transform body and soul. In the creativity cycle,
after you activate an idea in the East and nurture it in the South,
you then experiment with it in the West. To put an idea into form,
you need to see what works and what doesn't work. In order to do
this, you must experiment with an idea, watching it change and
go through various transformations.

The Spirit of the North

As you complete the circle, you arrive in the North. In the cycle
of life, the North is the realm of winter, the darkest night, and the
dark of the moon. It's also completion and consolidation. In the
human cycle the North is associated with the achievement of maturity, the accomplishments of the middle years of life, and the transition to old age, the elders, and the grandmothers and grandfathers.
The North is also the realm of death and rebirth. The colors of the
North are the stark white and black of winter. The medicine power
of the North is wisdom and introspection. There's a powerful inner
knowing that comes from being connected to the earth.

The element that dwells in the North of the medicine wheel is
earth, which symbolizes the physical aspects of self. Earth energy
is grounding, allowing you to stand your ground in times of adver-
sity. Earth is not only the surface of the ground that you can see,

such as the mountains, hills, boulders, rocks, and stones, but also the depth of the soil deep beneath your feet. Additionally, Earth includes those things that have roots firmly embedded in it, such as trees and plants. In the cycle of creativity, after you activate an idea in the East, nurture it in the South, and experiment with it in the West, you consolidate it in the North. The North is also the place of ancient wisdom. The key word for the North is *introspection*.

The animal spirits in the North are bear and turtle. Both hibernate in the winter and go into the darkness. The bear, a dramatic symbol in myth and lore because of its power and speed (up to 40 miles per hour for short distances), is the masculine aspect of the earth. The turtle is the feminine aspect. In the Far East, the turtle's shell is a symbol of heaven and the underside is a symbol of the earth; thus, the turtle represents blessings from heaven and earth. In some Native America traditions, the turtle is associated with the lunar cycle, feminine principles, and is a symbol of Mother Earth.

Following are the different aspects of the Medicine Wheel:

	East	South	West	North
Quality	mental	emotional	spiritual	physical
Element	air	water	fire	earth
Season	spring	summer	autumn	winter
Sun	dawn	noon	sunset	midnight
Moon	waxing moon	full moon	waning moon	new moon
Color	yellow/green	blue	red	black/white
Human	birth	childhood	young adult	elder
Creativity	activation	nurturance	experimentation	consolidation
Key Word	inspiration	intuition	transformation	introspection
Animals	eagle/owl	frog/dolphin	phoenix/snake	bear/turtle

There are fundamental energy differences between the Northern Hemisphere and the Southern that will affect your medicine wheel. However, it's easy to adapt your medicine wheel to the Southern Hemisphere. Energy moves clockwise in the Northern Hemisphere and counterclockwise in the Southern Hemisphere; therefore, it's appropriate to travel the wheel in a counterclockwise manner in the Southern Hemisphere. In the Northern Hemisphere the North is home of the winter, cold, and darkness; however, in the Southern Hemisphere the South is the home of winter. Therefore, the qualities of the North and the South in the medicine wheel are reversed in the Southern Hemisphere.

The Medicine Wheel
Northern Hemisphere

North
Season: winter
Element: earth
Aspect: physical
Expression: wisdom, integration, pragmatism, consolidation, evaluation
Spirit Keeper: bear (m), turtle (f)
Human Cycle: elder, grandmother, grandfather
Creativity: review and evaluation
Color: black/white
Mineral: smoky quartz

West
Season: autumn
Element: fire
Aspect: spiritual
Expression: transformation, illumination
Spirit Keeper: phoenix (m), snake (f)
Human Cycle: adolescence, young adult
Creativity: form, trial and error
Color: red
Mineral: clear quartz

East
Season: spring
Element: air
Aspect: mental
Expression: intellect, thought, communication
Spirit Keeper: eagle (m), owl (f)
Human Cycle: birth
Creativity: new beginnings, activation, inspiration
Color: yellow/green
Mineral: citrine

South
Season: summer
Element: water
Aspect: emotional
Expression: emotions, feelings, nurturing, innocence, humility
Spirit Keeper: frog (m), dolphin (f)
Human Cycle: childhood
Creativity: development, nurture, protect
Color: blue
Mineral: amethyst

Southern Hemisphere

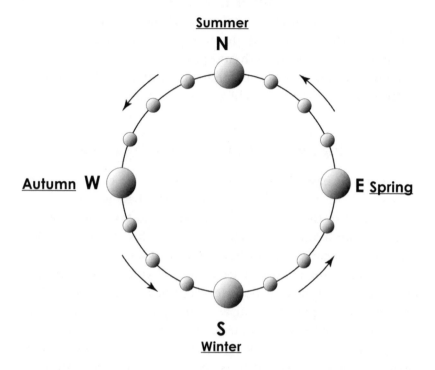

Summer
N

Autumn W ... **E Spring**

S
Winter

The Location of Your Circle

It's important to decide the general location for the circle for your Quest ahead of time. Traditionally, a person on a Vision Quest would look for a spot that was elevated and had a good view. However, the best place for your Vision Quest is the place that feels best to you. Each kind of terrain offers its own special qualities. For example, if you decide to have your Vision Quest in a valley, cave, or canyon, it can offer energy that feels womblike, comforting, and protected, and can contribute to focusing your attention inward.

An elevated place can have the advantage of allowing you to gain a wider perspective of your life. When you are able to see far in all directions, it's a metaphor for seeing all directions in your life.

The kinds of vegetation and terrain around your circle will contribute to your experience. Sitting in a desert can feel purifying and expanding. A Quest under tall trees on soft moss can feel nurturing and supportive. A strong oak tree near your circle can help you to tap into your innate strength and power. A creek flowing nearby can bring the qualities of inspiration and intuition. Take time to do a little research to find the right general area for you.

Finding the Specific Location for Your Quest

After you have decided the general area for your quest, the next step is to find the exact location. The best way to do this is to first go to the area you have chosen and take some time to still your mind and relax. When you are relaxed your intuition becomes stronger. Turn slowly in all directions and see if there's one particular direction that seems to pull you. Walk slowly and deliberately in that direction, feeling relaxed and at ease. The more effort you put into your walk and the more that you "try" to find the right location, the more difficult it becomes. Just relax. Breathe deeply. Enjoy being in nature. Don't consciously decide where you want to go, just walk in a natural way as if you were going on a wonderful afternoon stroll. This kind of walking will usually direct you to the perfect spot for your Quest.

The next step is to locate the exact center for your circle. To do this, stand in the area you have chosen, close your eyes, and notice what you are feeling. Do you feel comfortable? Do you feel energized and strong? Then move a few feet away and do the same thing. As you continue this process, by elimination you will discover the exact center of your circle that is best for you.

Sometimes the search for the location of your Quest can be as enlightening as the Vision Quest itself. Jaap de Kreek, a Dutch advertising executive, wrote to me about his search for his Quest location:

*I had known the spot for more than 20 years. [In my medi-
tations and dreams I had seen] a sloping meadow surrounded
with high trees, giving a wide view over a bay. In the middle of
this stood one tree with its feet [roots] covered with soft moss. I
had seen this spot often when I was on the edge of falling asleep.
And when I was breaking through the bushes of Sacred Island,
looking for a place where I could create my Vision Circle, I saw
it again. But this time it was real. Right before my eyes . . . the
slope, the tree, the bay, the moss, exactly as I had dreamed it.
There even was already a beautiful circle of stones, just where
it ought to be. Damn! Somebody had already marked the place
as if it was their own. Well, I was prepared to fight for this spot
[that had appeared to me so often in my dreams].*

*Behind me I heard a timid "Hello." [I turned and saw] the
only woman in the group I didn't like. She had come to claim
this place that she had found the day before.*

*[I thought,] "The hell with you. I'm not going. I don't like
you. I'm not giving up." Once again, a woman wants to send me
away. Angry emotions flashed through me. And then suddenly,
I had a realization. I recognized that I had the opportunity to
release an old emotional pattern regarding women. In that moment, I decided to let the woman have "my" spot.*

*[I thought to myself,] "Woman, I don't like you. I will never
like you, but you gave me a present. You offered me the chance
to look straight through myself to my ego."*

*I walked back into the bushes. In a small basin was a boul-
der, broken into two pieces. There I wanted to sit for a while and
recuperate from the shock. While my thoughts still heaved on
the waves of my emotions, I saw that the boulder and I were
surrounded by trees. Behind the branches glimmered the bay.*

*Two years later [I decided to go] to Sacred Island for my
second Vision Quest. [I thought,] "Now I can finally take the
opportunity to take possession of my dream spot for my Quest."
At last I was sitting on the moss. My moss. I was happy. Then
behind me I heard a timid "Halloo." A shy lady asked me if*

there was by chance another good spot in the area where she could create her Vision Circle.

"No, there's none," I told her with certainty. I could see the disappointment in her eyes. Then I heard another voice [come out of my mouth and] say, "But if you want, you can take this one." I couldn't believe it. Was it really me who said this?

While she was positioning herself on the spot that I knew by heart, I leaned on a broken boulder and slowly and contentedly felt myself melt into the womb of Mother Earth.

It's valuable to observe the thoughts, feelings, and experiences you have while finding your spot. They can be significant and can give you powerful insights into yourself. Mervi Jakonen, a podiatrist from Finland, wrote to me about finding her location and what she gained from the search:

I panicked when I tried to find the right place for my Quest. You had advised me to look for the signs but I didn't see any. When I had asked you, "How much time do I have to find my place?" you said, "How much do you need?" [I couldn't find my place and] I was desperate when I realized that I had only one hour before dark to find my spot.

I went to the forest, talked to the trees, and asked them to help me. Nothing happened. I ran through the woods, talking to myself, knowing that I had to find some place. Then I gave up. Suddenly I realized what you really meant. It wasn't about finding the "place," it was about finding "when" I was ready. As soon as I had this realization, I went straight to my place. I felt peace at that moment . . . and also a little bit stupid for tearing around through the woods. I had wanted a Vision Quest spot that was close to the sea and near a big tree so that I could see the sunset and the clear sky at night. As soon as I was ready, my spot appeared. It was easy.

You do not need to struggle to find the perfect place. When you can still your mind, as Mervi did, and find sacred space inside yourself, it becomes easy to find sacred space outside yourself.

The earth has a living force within it. Your life force is constantly interacting with the living spirit within the earth. There are places on the earth where you are strengthened and places where you are weakened. They're not the same for everyone. Once, a woman wanted to take me to her sacred spot in nature. She was very excited about showing it to me. We hiked for roughly a mile and then had to push through dense vegetation for about 20 minutes. Finally we broke out of the brush into a small opening. A tree with thick foliage and low-hanging branches created a shady covering over a small area that had a very small spring flowing through it. When we arrived, her entire energy field expanded and she looked the most vibrant and radiant that I had ever seen her. I could see that the land was sustaining her. However, my energy began to dip and sag until I was exhausted and had difficulty making my way back down the trail. The location on the land that energized her depleted me. It wasn't a bad spot or a good spot. It just interacted with her energy in a different way than it did with mine.

Creating Your Sacred Circle

Usually the medicine wheel circle for a Vision Quest is made from stones, but it can also be created from the materials in the surrounding area, perhaps twigs or sticks or pinecones if there are no stones. Sometimes a circle is made of four twigs stuck upright in the earth with pieces of colored cloth tied to them to represent the four directions. In some traditions, tobacco is used to help create the sacred circle. It's used in many Native American ceremonies, for it's thought to be a medium of communication with the unseen ones and is sacred to the Creator in all its forms. Vision seekers place a small pinch of tobacco in the center of a one- to two-inch square of cloth, which is tied with string to make a small pouch. Bundles of these are tied together and strung around the periphery of the sacred Vision Quest circle. This helps to sanctify and energize the circle. There are many different ways and different materials to use to create your wheel; however, the materials that are used for your medicine wheel are less important than the respect you give to the entire process.

The Power of Stones in a Medicine Wheel

Ancient medicine men and women understood the power of stones and often used them in ceremonies and rituals because they believed that they contained living spirits with healing properties. Though rocks seem inanimate, they were thought to be no less alive than a wild rose opening to the morning sun or a deer grazing in a mountain meadow. Even the most guarded skeptic cannot deny the feeling created by the stones and rocks in their environment. Who isn't moved by the power exuding from a magnificent boulder perched high on an ocean cliff as it defies harsh north winds? And who hasn't felt comforted just by holding a water-worn stone that fits so perfectly in one's hand?

Creating your medicine wheel with stones will give your circle a sense of strength, stability, and groundedness. The way that you search for the stones and how you relate to those stones are very important. In order to understand why stones are used, it helps to gain a perspective of the energy available within the mineral kingdom. Some native peoples believe there's a living spirit in each stone, and they call these stones and rocks "stone people."

In many aspects, Taoist philosophy mirrors the Native American kinship with stones. Kio Jo-hsu, a Taoist Chinese painter in the T'ang Dynasty said:

> He who is learning to paint must first still his heart, thus to clarify his understanding and increase his wisdom. In stilling the heart an individual can become one with the elements of nature, the great creative forces of the Tao and its processes. To clarify understanding and increase wisdom means a contemplative attention to all of nature's changes in order gradually to gain a sense of the permanent and significant. In estimating people, their quality of spirit (chi) is as basic as the way they are

formed; and so it is with rocks, which are the framework of the heavens and of earth, and also have chi. This is the reason rocks are sometimes spoken of as "roots of the clouds."[1]

Native and ancient people saw a world beyond the material and the tangible, and that is why they acknowledged the living spirit in rocks.

Where to Find Your Stones

It's best to collect stones from the area where you'll hold your Vision Quest; however, if there are no stones there, you may bring some from another place. But please don't take stones from sacred sites. For example, many people have traveled to the interior of Australia to visit a sacred aboriginal site, Ayers rock (called Uluru by the Aborigines), and have taken rocks back home with them. The Pitjantjatjara Aborigines people feel that these rocks belong to Uluru, which is a sacred "dreaming" site, and have requested that any stones taken be returned home. A Chinese painter, Lu Ch'ai, referred to the living spirit of stones when he said that there's a kinship among rocks: "Small rocks near water are like children gathered around with arms outstretched toward the mother rock. On a mountain there's a large rock, the elder, that seems to reach out and gather the children about him."

If you live near the sea you might comb the beaches for your stones. Stones that have been smoothed and polished by the motion of the surf carry power from the depths of the ocean. Their spirit speaks of wide expansive skies, deep blue sea, and the surging changes of surf and sand. The stones found inland have a completely different energy. Stones found near roots of trees or along the base of cliffs have the spirit of the ancient land. Their spirit carries the richness of the dark loam of Mother Earth and her primordial secrets. Stones found in inland riverbeds and streams carry the fluid flowing energy of water as well as the strength of the earth. Every stone carries the energy of its past and the area where it's found.

How to Choose Your Stones

Each stone affects your energy field in a different way. When you randomly pick up a stone from the earth, you're intuitively tapping into the inherent beneficial energy within it. Each stone that you choose from your sacred circle affects the energy of the circle in a specific and unique way. As strange as it might sound, when you find stones for your medicine wheel, it's important to first ask their permission to take them. There's a subtle yet powerful balance of energy on our planet and the mineral realm is an important contribution to that balance. Even changing the location of one stone can affect the pattern of energy flows throughout the land. Some stones need to stay where they are, so it's important to ask if it's all right to take a stone. Even if you feel a bit silly, as you hold your stone, tap into your intuition and imagine that you're carrying on a dialogue with the stone. Asking permission can be as simple as closing your eyes and asking, "May I take you for my medicine wheel?" When the response comes, honor it. I find that most stones accept the invitation.

Whenever you move a stone from one place to another, inwardly acknowledge to the stone why it's being taken from its living place (this also helps you clarify your intention for your retreat). In addition, it's important when you take a stone for your sacred circle to leave an offering such as tobacco or corn meal or some token of thanks. I know of a Blackfoot Indian who leaves shiny copper pennies when he takes something from nature. Though this is not low-impact camping ("take only pictures, leave only footprints"), it gives credence to the native tradition of honoring that which is taken from nature. If you have nothing tangible to leave, offer thoughts or words of thanks and gratitude. If possible, return your stones to the location where you found them after you have completed your Vision Quest.

Trance Walk to Find Medicine Wheel Stones

When I was young, I was taught a particular kind of walking done by my Cherokee ancestors that I call Trance Walk. It's a valuable technique to use if you're having difficulty locating your stones. To Trance Walk to locate stones, stand with both feet stable and firm on the earth. You can wear shoes while doing this, if you want, although it's important to feel an emotional or energetic connection to the earth. Begin taking very deep full breaths that center in your lower abdomen. This means when you inhale your abdomen expands, and when you exhale your abdomen contracts. As you continue these breaths, lower your eyelids, leaving them open just enough that you can still see. Then place your awareness in your diaphragm area as you hold an intention of gathering stones for your circle. By doing this you're putting out the "call" to be led to just the right stones.

Some people say they feel a sensation like a tug or pull on their diaphragm area, and others just find themselves walking without any conscious decision to do so. As you walk, hold the thought of the particular qualities of the stone that you want to use for your wheel. For example, if you're looking for a stone to place in the South (which represents water) of your wheel, spend a moment connecting to the element of water, then say within yourself, *Spirit of the South, Spirit of Water, direct me to a stone that will help me connect to the element of water during my Quest.* Sometimes it will seem that a stone is beckoning to you or sometimes it will look shinier or brighter than the stones around it. I've seen stones that even seemed to glow from within, and I knew that they would bring power and grace into my circle.

It's a good idea to obtain the four cardinal stones first. Thus, the first stone will call forth the Spirit of the East, followed by the Spirits of the South, West, and North. Once you have your four directional stones, you can Trance Walk for the remaining stones.

Feeling a Connection with Your Stones

Once you have chosen your "stone people," spend time with them before laying them in your circle, to understand and feel their strength and energy. It's possible to enter into the consciousness of these special rocks. Entering the awareness of animate and inanimate objects is one of the secrets of the shaman. Using methods similar to those of ancient mystic travelers, you can tap into the spirit power of stones. It's important to do this before you create your sacred circle, for it brings you into closer communication and harmony with the stones that will form it.

To experience the living spirit within a stone, hold it in front of you. Really look at it. Observe the mountains and valleys of its surface. Feel the textures and temperatures as you explore the surface with your fingers. Close your eyes and feel every corner and crevice of the stone. Breathe deeply, still your mind, and imagine that you're entering into the center of the stone. As you embark on this imaginary journey, notice how you feel as you penetrate into the core of the stone. Do you feel still and strong? Do you feel powerful and expansive? Every rock has a different energy and will allow you a different experience.

Now imagine that you're actually becoming the stone and observe how it feels. Every stone is a unique spirit with a particular vibration of light and sound and its own story to tell. For example, a quartz crystal has a very different energy than a granite riverbed stone, and turquoise is very different from obsidian. Quartz is light, bright, and has a transmitting energy. A riverbed stone is grounding and strong. Turquoise is porous and flowing, whereas obsidian is dense, solid, and intense. Let yourself imagine or be aware of the story that dwells within each stone. Native American healers knew how to speak to stones and what particular influence each stone would have. They chose specific stones that created beneficial effects for the purposes that they desired.

When you're surrounded by the stones that you've chosen for your Quest, these "stone people" stand around you like silent guardians with their ancient wisdom and timeless strength. It's important that you feel safe and protected for your Quest. The stones you've made friends with, and feel a connection to, will help create a circle of power around you. The stone people become your friends and companions through the day and night. They will stand guard over you bringing their rich grounding connection to Mother Earth while you're on your Quest.

Constructing Your Sacred Circle

The center of all medicine wheels is symbolic of the Creator, so the center of your circle is important. Sometimes the center is immediately apparent, sometimes you may need to spend time using your intuition to "feel" where the exact spot is. Once you have decided the center, it's important to declare your intention. For example, you might say, "May Grandmother Earth below and Grandfather Sky above fill this place with energy and love as I create my Sacred Circle for my Vision Quest." Sprinkle a little cornmeal (which symbolizes protection and abundance) or tobacco (which is sacred to the Creator) and give a prayer of thanks in the center of your circle.

If you want your circle to be fairly accurate geometrically, here's a way to do it. Put a stick into earth in the center of your circle. Attach to your stick a string or cord half the length of the diameter of your circle. For example, if you want a six-foot circle, tie a three-foot string to the stick. Then attach another stick to the other end of the string and use it to etch the circumference in the dirt. This will make your medicine wheel an exact circle. It's not necessary, however, to make your medicine wheel a perfect circle. Some terrains make it very difficult to create. The most important thing is to acknowledge within yourself that your sacred circle, no matter what form or shape, is symbolic of the sacred circles within all life.

Make your circle bigger than your height so that you can comfortably lie down in it. (I like to use an eight-to-ten-foot diameter.) One Vision Quester inadvertently made her circle smaller than her height, so she could only sit up in it rather than lie down.

After a day of this, she realized that in life she was always creating self-limiting situations for herself and then complaining about her self-imposed confines. She decided to make a new template for her life and so remade her circle so that she could move and lie down in it with ease. With this symbolic act, she realized that she could create a life for herself that was freer and less confined.

After you have decided on the shape, the next step is to clear the space. If there are small stones or sticks within the circle, clear them out. In the creation of your circle, every act is sacred. Build your circle with awareness and reverence. Once the area is cleared, ascertain what direction is East. You can do this with a compass; if you don't have a compass, the easiest way is to establish where the sun rises.

The ceremony of creating the circle brings power and clarity into your life. As you lay each stone or twig in your medicine wheel, you are enacting a ritual. When you call the elements into your circle, you are honoring the different cycles in your life. Start by taking the stone that symbolizes the East and ask that the Spirit of Air and the Spirit of the East fill your sacred circle. Place this stone in the easternmost spot of the perimeter of your circle. Step back and feel energy filling your circle. Continue by placing the South stone, followed by the West stone and the North stone. With each step, be aware that not only are you creating a physical circle, you're creating a circle of energy. Each step of the creation process calls power into your circle.

Your four cardinal stones represent the four elements and the four directions. These are laid out to form the perimeter of the circle. Allow equal space between each of the four major stones. In between these major stones, position your other stones, using as many as feel best to you. Remember, however, that each stone you place around the perimeter is bringing a very special energy into your circle. Each stone represents the transition from one quadrant of your life to another. The stone circle represents the pathway from one aspect of your life to another. Your placement of the stones is an affirmation that the transitions in your life are easy and flowing.

Take as much time as you need when setting up your wheel. This is a sacred place, so treat the circle with respect. You're creating a womb or cocoon of energy with every aspect of the creation of your circle. When your circle is complete, stand back from it and see if it feels right. If it doesn't, take time to make whatever adjustments are needed until it does feel right.

When you have finished, give thanks. Thank the earth for providing such a special place for your Quest. Thank the surrounding vegetation and trees for giving loving support for your Quest. Ask for assistance from the Living Spirit in the surrounding area and give thanks for the beauty and love that's given from nature and from the realm of Spirit.

For some, the creation of the medicine wheel can be as meaningful as the Vision Quest itself. Rick Mauricio, a lighting technician from Great Britain, had a vision while seeking and creating his power spot:

> *The Vision Quest for me was very much about finding my purpose in this life. . . . I allowed myself to be drawn deep into the wood to find my spot. Once I reached a particular place, I found I could not advance past it in any direction. I didn't like the place. The air was thick with mosquitoes, flies and bugs, but everything pointed to this being the place for me. Even though the area was filled with bushes and undergrowth, I had a feeling that this was where I was meant to be. The air was teeming with bugs, but the moment I created my sacred circle, all the insects stayed outside it! In fact, none entered until I dismantled my circle the next evening.*
>
> *Once I stepped inside my circle I felt what seemed to be a powerful energy emitting up from the earth. It was just North of the center of the circle. It wasn't there before I created the circle, as I didn't feel it when I was clearing the ground. It must have emerged after the circle was complete. I was completely amazed by what I was feeling and moved my hand over the boundaries of the energy. Every time my hand got near it, I could feel a tingling in my fingers and palm.*

To try to understand what was occurring, I dropped a leaf over the spot. The leaf swayed and danced in the air and then eventually fell. I rationalized that the leaf could have caught a breeze so I decided to try a twig. The same thing happened. Again I rationalized that the twig was light so maybe it was a breeze that caused it to seem to hang in the air. I then tried a stone. Remarkably, the stone also danced and swayed and didn't land in the place it should have.

Dusk was approaching. I lay down next to the earth to see if I could understand what could cause this unusual phenomenon. In the failing light, I saw a few small stones near the energy spot. I picked them up and moved them around in the palm of my hand. They began to emit light! As I stared closer at them in my hand, I started to see them as stars. As the remaining daylight disappeared, I looked up and I could see a point of light through the trees. As I looked closer it looked like a great circle of light, almost like a medicine wheel.

There were points along the circumference that had bursts of light shooting in and out of the circle, like the points of a medicine wheel. I realized these shifting patterns of light represented the changes in my life. As the points lengthened and shortened, changing themselves, I realized that I could change myself. I then had the profound realization that we can change anything and everything in a twinkling of an eye. It was at that point that my name came to me . . . Shifting Star. It's both who I am and what I'm capable of. This was a momentous moment in my life. The energy vortex in my sacred circle, the glowing stones, and shifting light were all gifts to me that showed me the limitless possibilities of being here on Mother Earth in this life. The most reassuring aspect to arise since my Vision Quest is that the way I respond to my world is always changing and I with it. Each day and moment is a Vision Quest for me.

Tessa Dace, a developer for affordable housing in South Africa, talked about the beauty of the creation of her circle:

I slowly set about the ritual of forming my circle. Selecting a large rock I spoke first to the East, and [dedicated the rock to] the air, the spring, mental thought, and the gateway to my circle. I asked for help in my Quest for inner knowledge, as I ceremoniously placed the rock on the ground. [I placed] another rock in the South, for the summer, the water, and emotions. I knew I would need assistance here! I placed another rock for the West, for fire, for autumn, and for energy beneath the handsome sturdy pine with its strong masculine trunk. A last stone I placed beneath a wizened old tree at the North, symbolizing earth, winter, and abundance. The spaces between I filled with smaller rocks, pieces of driftwood, and bark, each placed with reverence in my private ceremony.

Addressing all my relations, in the Native American custom, I entered my circle from the East and lay down on the moss bed. My precious drum, so newly finished, hung to dry next to my head. I could almost hear the deep voice it would have. My dream catcher, sage bundle, and tobacco pouch became an impromptu altar. Feeling the words I had just spoken in my sacred ceremony so very close to my heart, I stared out to sea.

Preparing to Enter Your Circle

Prior to entering your medicine wheel, purify and consecrate yourself by "smudging." Smudging, or sage cleansing, is a sacred ritual used for purification and preparation for ceremonies. To smudge, carefully light a sage bundle (if you do not have a sage bundle you may use incense), take the smoke in your hands, and "wash" it over your hair and head (to think only pure thoughts), eyes (to see the truth), ears (to hear the truth), throat (to speak with clarity and truth), and heart (to give and receive love freely). Be very careful to avoid fire danger. If you're doing your Quest without matches or sage, take your hands and repeat the same symbolic "washing" motions but without the smoke. (Important:

in an area of high fire risk don't use matches or make a fire or smoke.) A symbolic smudging can be as potent as an actual one using smoking herbs, if done with intent and love. There's power in symbolic gestures.

Before entering your circle, hold in your mind's eye your overall intention for your Quest. Taking your time to concentrate on your intention for your Quest is important. Perhaps you desire to gain clarity about your future path, or want to resolve a relationship, or wish to evaluate a career decision. Where intention goes, energy flows, so placing your intention on the area in your life you wish to change will help energy flow in that direction.

After you have focused your intent for your Quest, offer a prayer to the Creator, asking for a blessing during your Quest. The best prayers come straight from your heart, honestly and sincerely. This is a very holy time. You are literally calling Spirit into your circle; calling your spirit helpers, guides, guardians, and angels to surround and fill your circle. When you have finished with your prayers, give thanks to the Creator.

Entering Your Medicine Wheel

The beginning of the wheel is the East (because the sun rises in the East), so always enter and leave the wheel through its eastern portion. When you set foot in your circle you may immediately notice a difference between the energy inside and outside, because you are entering a vortex of energy that has been created by careful attention and love. Many times Vision Questers have recounted stories of watching animals approach their circle and then carefully walk around the perimeter, even when the stones were so small as not to differentiate the area. Your medicine wheel is a sacred space where you can interface with the universe, and animals can often feel this.

Candace created a beautiful medicine wheel for her Quest. It was in the center of a large meadow in the Cascade Mountains. There weren't any large rocks in the area so she gathered gravel-sized stones to create her circle. On the second day of her Quest, she had to go to a spring to get more water. It was some distance from her circle so she was gone about an hour. When she returned she saw numerous hoof marks of range cattle completely surrounding her circle, yet not one hoof mark was inside her circle. The cattle had intuitively felt the energy of her sacred space and respected it. Other people on Quests have had the experience of certain animals being attracted to the energy of their medicine circles. Sometimes an animal entering your circle might be the bearer of a message, which could be a part of your vision. The energy you create by your intention in building your circle, both conscious and unconscious, helps to determine what will happen. The important thing is to be open to all the signs and information that come to you.

Once you have entered your medicine wheel, either sit or stand in the center and take a moment to be still. Listen. Close your eyes and take seven deep breaths (one breath for each direction, one breath for the energy above, one for the energy below, and one for the center or the Creator). Take as much time as you like to center yourself and become deeply relaxed. Face the East and allow yourself to feel a connection to the Spirit of the East. Shift positions to face each quadrant: East, South, West, and North. (In the Southern Hemisphere face East, North, West, and South.) Hold the intention for your Quest within your thoughts. As you face each cardinal point, imagine drawing energy from that quadrant; focus and examine your intent from the perspective and power of each direction.

Absorb and perceive the power of the direction you face. It may manifest itself as light, color, sound, an insight, or a feeling. When finished with each direction, return your awareness to the center of the circle. Feel the energies from each direction spiraling toward the middle of the wheel; in this vortex of energy, send your prayers up to Spirit. You can now bring everything that you're going to use on your Quest into the circle, such your sleeping bag and water. (Remember to enter and leave through the East.) Every time you cross over the threshold, say, "I do this for the good of all beings," as a way to remind yourself of the value of what you are doing. Some individuals say, "To all my relations," which is a similar sentiment. You are now ready to begin your Quest.

Gael Edmeades, a Reiki master from South Africa, wrote about creating her circle:

> *The day we all had been waiting for was almost upon us. Morning dawned and it was raining! Groaning silently to myself at the thought of sitting out there in the rain for two days but, ever resourceful, making a quick raid on the kitchen for black plastic bags which were to be used as roof and ground sheet, I prepared my medicine wheel. My spot was a circle within a circle of stones within a circle of trees. What could be more magical than that? I set out my stones and feathers to mark the South, West, North and then closed the East after inviting the ancestors and guardians in. I lay down on my stomach in the middle of my medicine wheel and felt every bone and muscle and sinew dissolve as I blended with the healing power of the earth. I had no boundaries, neither physical, mental, nor emotional, and I felt the heartbeat of the earth . . . and I was one with it.*

Creating a Medicine Wheel Indoors

Though Questing in nature can bring a wonderful dimension to your retreat, not everyone has the opportunity or inclination to do so. Therefore, you can create a Quest indoors. Your medicine wheel can be created using the preceding information for finding and placing your stones, or you can make your indoor circle with special objects. For example, because of health concerns, one woman decided to create her medicine wheel indoors. She had collected a number of feathers over the years and decided to use them to make her circle. She took the feathers and, through a process of meditation, decided which of them should be placed in the positions of East, South, West, and North. After this, she used the remainder of the feathers to create the circle, in much the same way as smaller "stepping-stones" are used in a stone circle. She had a very successful Quest and afterward said that she had felt that her circle was surrounded by the wings of angels.

Rocks or twigs can be brought in from outdoors to create an indoor sacred circle. Evergreen boughs and needles may also be used to form the wheel. Whatever objects have significance for you, and are readily available, can be used for this purpose, using the steps outlined above.

In today's world, sacred space is being forgotten. However, deep within the recesses of the mind is a primal memory of the power of the sacred circle. That ancient, though elusive, memory has the ability to activate a conditioned response that connects you to the majesty of past Quests. It's an act of power to create sacred circles, which help to remind us how to live in a sacred way. The medicine wheel can take you back in safety to the simplest forms of living. It also can bring you back lovingly to the present, without the complexity of society's ideas of what you need in order to be full and complete; those qualities are gained within the context of the circle. Casting the sacred circle can help remind you of who you are and why you are here. This is the majesty of the Quest within the circle.

CHAPTER FOUR

WHAT DO YOU DO
ON A VISION QUEST?

Your needs, as well as what you hope to achieve on your Quest, will help determine what you do on your Quest. Some Quests may be aimed at addressing various aspects of life and have a specific agenda. For someone who is very goal oriented, this kind of Quest may be just one more thing to cross off on the "To-Do List" of life. For this kind of individual sometimes the best thing to do on a Vision Quest is *nothing*. Just sit. Just *be*. There's nothing you have to do or accomplish. Be still. Surrender. Watch. Listen. Feel. Move toward acceptance of absolutely everything that occurs. Be the observer. Be in the present moment without judgment or expectations and without trying to accomplish anything.

For other types of individuals, the way to self-discovery is to have a direction or focus for the Vision Quest. If you are one of those individuals, I have created the following five-step journey to use as a guideline for your time alone in nature:

1. Examine your life

2. Face your fears and release your attachments

3. Tap into the spirit power within you

4. Give thanks

5. Call for a vision

Step 1. Examine Your Life

Relive Your Life

Go through your entire life remembering, experiencing, and accepting as much as you can. (You may want to write it all down in a journal.) Try to remember every possible detail of your life, starting from early childhood though to the present. If you have trouble remembering details from some period, simply jot down what you can remember. Doing this often primes the pump so that more memories come flowing out to fill in the gaps. Don't get stuck in any one place. Just recall as much as you can and keep going. Review your past actions and pay particular attention to your feelings. If you find yourself getting bogged down in an old emotional pattern, become the observer. Try to observe the situation from an impartial viewpoint.

On her Quest, Janice spent half a day reliving her anger at her older sister. She thought over and over again: *I'll never forgive her. Never. Never!* Although there's value in bringing repressed emotions to the surface, sometimes negative emotions can be like a scratched CD that keeps playing the same words over and over again. Janice kept repeating the scenario in her mind, which wasn't productive. I suggested that she observe the situation from a detached perspective. When she did this, she was able to understand not only the situation with her sister but a series of relationship patterns in her life.

EXERCISE: WITNESS YOUR LIFE

Reexperience your life in its totality and at the same time watch it unfold. Become the objective witness. Don't judge; just observe. Notice patterns that continue to recur during your life. Notice recurring issues. What has been really significant in your life?

When you look back at your life, often there are only a few things that really stand out. Sometimes it seems as if the rest of the time has been spent waiting for those things to happen. It's not usually our monumental projects and great plans of which the real stuff of life is made. Often it's the space between these events, the ordinary, everyday moments of life, that contain the crucial and potent moments of soul. These are often the moments from which our definitions of self arise.

EXERCISE: TURNING POINTS IN LIFE

What are the main events in your life? Do you spend your time waiting for the future, rather than living each moment fully? What are the turning points in your life?

Find Your Essence; Discover Your Theme

There's a prevailing theme that runs through your life, just as there's a prevalent essence of you that has woven its way through your personal history. What has your life's theme been? What is the unique essence of you?

Sandy, a florist from Utah, detailed her life history in a journal she took on her Quest. As she wrote, she began to notice a lifelong pattern of relationships in which she felt smothered by the affection of others and was constantly fighting for her freedom. As she explored her life's theme, she realized that freedom was extraordinarily important to her; the theme of her entire life was based on gaining physical, emotional, and spiritual freedom. When she examined the moments in her life that were truly important to her, they all seemed to carry a theme of freedom. Each major incident in her life revolved around freedom: the time when she got in a fight with her parents about getting her driver's license, the time that she picketed a government building for suppressing freedom of the press, and the time her boyfriend wanted her to exclude other friends from her life.

As she further explored her life, she wanted to find her essence. She asked her inner voice, *What is my essence?* This is what she heard: "I heard an inner voice speak clearly: *You are Truth*. When I said the words to myself, *I am Truth*, I felt fantastic. I knew I had touched my essence." Sandy realized that when she spoke her "truth," she was "free." One's essence manifests through the theme of one's life; therefore, Sandy's essence (truth) was manifested through her life theme of freedom.

EXERCISE: WHAT IS YOUR THEME?

What is your essence? What is the theme of your life? What is unique about you? What have been the consistent motifs throughout your experiences? What do you constantly struggle with? In what area of your life do you continually gain your triumphs?

Consequences of Your Life Choices and Your Probable Future

Every act creates consequences. Even the simple act of tossing a small stone into a lake can potentially affect the outcome of history. (The stone could startle a large fish, which swims into a net, which is caught by the fisherman, who takes it home to his village clan leader, who invites the neighboring clan leader for a fish meal, who chokes on a fish bone, which starts a war, which affects the course of history.) Don't let the fact that your actions have consequences inhibit you from taking action in your life. Just do the best you can. Even the smallest act taken with a loving heart can make a big impact in your life. Set your sights on the direction in which you want to walk, and to the best of your ability walk that path. Then relax and know that your life is working out the way it should. (Don't worry if all your acts aren't pure hearted—no one is completely loving. Most of your mistakes aren't going to cause catastrophes!) Take responsibility for your actions, but don't get bogged down in guilt or fear.

Because you are in a circle of power, the small positive steps that you take during your Vision Quest can have a dramatic effect on your future. All life is interdependent, and every act creates a ripple in the fabric of time. Everything you think or do sets your future in motion. Every single thought and action has an effect on your future or has a result in your life. You *can* re-create your future during the Vision Quest. During your Quest you can set an energy in motion that can literally alter the course of your probabilities and even change your destiny.

EXERCISE: PROBABILITY PATTERN OF YOUR FUTURE

Given your past thoughts and actions, what's your current destiny? In your imagination, project yourself into your future. Given the probabilities of your history, and given your subconscious programming, what's in store for your future? Contemplate traveling to your probable future: one year, five years, seven years, ten years, twenty, thirty, forty, and beyond. Are you happy with what you see? Do you feel satisfied with the probability patterns of your future?

Go forward in time to just before your death. Imagine yourself sitting in a rocking chair looking back on your life. Are there any regrets? What changes would you make? People very rarely regret what they did do but often regret what they didn't do. What would you change if you could do it all over again? Is there anything in your present life you need to change to restructure your potential future? Examine how that change will alter every aspect of your life, and make sure you are at peace with that. If you see anything in your probable future with which you're uncomfortable, picture it dissolving and then imagine how you can create the future you desire.

Examine Your Relationships

Relationship to Self: Your Beliefs. It's enormously valuable to examine the relationships in your life, starting with your relationship with yourself. To discover the dynamics of this, begin by examining your beliefs. One of the most dynamic configurations of thought is a belief. A belief is a concept that you consider to be the truth. It can dictate the way you think and feel and can even affect the way you act. Your personal beliefs can cause you to attract particular situations and circumstances into your life. Whatever you believe has consequences. In fact, your beliefs can determine the outcome of your life.

"Core" beliefs are more influential than ordinary beliefs. They're beliefs that are generally so deep-seated that you're not even conscious of them, yet they have a tremendous effect on your life. They're so instilled in you that they become a part of your "ground of being," rather like gravity, which you usually don't question or think about. It's just "the way it is."

Subconsciously, we're constantly trying to validate our core beliefs. We feel the need to be "right" about these beliefs so we subconsciously create a reality to justify our beliefs . . . *even if the beliefs are negative.* For example, Emilio had a core belief that dogs were dangerous. Even though consciously he realized that most dogs were not a problem, whenever he went for a walk, dogs inevitably barked at him. He subconsciously projected fear whenever he approached a dog. Consequently, dogs sensed his fear and often reacted negatively to Emilio. This repeated unpleasant experience validated his deep inner belief that dogs are dangerous. Ron presents another example. Consciously, he really enjoyed the company of women; however, every time he became intimate with a woman, she would betray his trust. While examining his life, Ron realized that this pattern had recurred through the years. Though he *consciously* believed that he could be intimate with woman, he realized that he had a strong core belief that women couldn't be trusted. His inner belief was so strong that he was subconsciously attracted to untrustworthy women . . . because they validated his inner belief.

EXERCISE: WHAT ARE YOUR BELIEFS?

List as many conscious beliefs as you can, taking time to discover where they may have originated (from a parent, friend, family member, society, and so on). Are you happy with your beliefs? Then list your core beliefs. The quickest way to discover your core beliefs is to observe the reality with which you have surrounded yourself. Given that your core beliefs create your reality, which core beliefs would explain the reality of your life?

After you have made your list, look it over and see if you are happy with all your core beliefs. What do your conscious beliefs and core beliefs tell you about your relationship to yourself?

In one of her Vision Quests, Trees had the opportunity to begin to recognize and release a fundamental negative belief that she had held for a long time:

The first day I drank a lot of water. The second day I put the container at the tree with my ribbon to indicate that I wanted more water. When the sun was at its highest I thought it was time for someone to come with water . . . but no water came. I prayed and sang . . . and after a long time I left my circle to see if someone had left water in my container by the tree . . . but still no water. I went back to my circle, crying all the way. In the past, every time I trusted someone, they betrayed me. They usually didn't do what they said they would do. I cried for a long time. It hurt so much.

Then I decided to leave my circle and go back to base camp to get water. I had to take action. I left my circle, checked the tree again, and went all the way to base camp. It was a long walk. I had never been so angry.

When I got back to base camp I learned that water had already been brought, but one of the assistants still came back with me with more fresh water. On the way back to my circle so much anger came out of me. The funny thing is that when we came back to the tree, the water was there, partially hidden by grass. In my circle I asked Great Spirit to forgive me for not trusting people. This lesson I will never forget. I also realized that I am responsible for myself.

When we're ready to release an old belief, we often go out of our way, subconsciously, to create a similar situation that will allow the belief to surface so that it can be released. Hence, even though there *was* water available, Trees subconsciously chose not to see it, so that her old belief of not trusting people could come to the surface.

When you sit in a sacred circle during your Quest, with no outside stimulus, it becomes much easier to see your belief patterns because there are fewer exterior circumstances to justify them. Normally when beliefs arise in our life, they seem real because there are external stimuli that seem to justify the beliefs. If you believe that the world is an angry place, you'll see angry people wherever you go, thus justifying your belief in an angry world. But if you're sitting in a circle of stones in nature feeling angry, it becomes more obvious where the emotion is coming from. Basically when you're in the circle, you're just sitting in a circle. Nothing more and nothing less. However, the sanctity of the circle offers the opportunity to *observe* your beliefs rather than act them out. Here are some thoughts and the underlying beliefs that have arisen on Vision Quests:

- *My circle isn't good enough. Everyone has a better circle than I do.* (*Belief:* Everyone is better than I am.)

- *My location is wrong. Why did I choose this location? Now I'm stuck with my choice.* (*Belief:* I never make the right choice.)

- *I'm sitting here all by myself feeling abandoned. Why have they abandoned me?* (*Belief:* I'll always be abandoned in life.)

- *I'm not doing my Vision Quest right.* (*Belief:* I never do anything right.)

- *This isn't working.* (*Belief:* Nothing ever works out for me.)

When you can observe a belief, rather than act on it, you can begin to loosen the hold that the belief has on you.

Gaining New Beliefs

You define yourself by your beliefs, and your life takes a "shape" that's determined by the beliefs you hold. When you adopt a belief system that's dictated from the outside, you're defined by another's form, and, like a shoe that's too small, it can pinch. During your Quest you have the opportunity to relinquish old limiting beliefs and embrace new beliefs that empower you. You can actually reengineer your consciousness. You have the opportunity to make radical changes in the thought patterns that have been running your life. You can do this by identifying your core beliefs, and then replacing them with more powerful ones. This is not a juxtaposing of one idea for another or an introduction of a new set of ideas into an old mind-set. It's actually a restructuring of the mind according to your conscious choice.

When you fully understand the beliefs that have been limiting you, you can begin to release them. For much of our lives we go around assuming that our underlying beliefs are an accurate reflection of reality, instead of just our own individual perceptions. However, once you explore your beliefs fully, then you're finally ready to release the ones that don't work and replace them with beliefs that support and empower you.

EXERCISE: RESTRUCTURING YOUR BELIEFS

As you discover your core beliefs, list them on the left half of a piece of paper. If you discover a belief that doesn't empower you, cross it out and next to it write a new core belief that is supportive and positive.

After you have written down your desired new beliefs, it's important to anchor them into your body and your subconscious. To do this, think of the new belief and imagine going into your body and finding a place that you might associate with this new belief. Place your left hand on that part of your body and imagine breathing into that part of your body at the same time as you are thinking of your new belief. This begins to imbed the new belief into your body. Every time you find the old limiting belief filtering back into your life, place your hand on that part of your body and repeat the exercise.

For example, if you want to anchor the belief that "I am a valuable person" into your energy field, you might choose your chest as the place in your body to anchor the belief. Place your left hand on your chest and think, "I am a valuable person." And then anytime that a thought of lack of esteem occurs, put your hand on your chest and say to yourself, "I am a valuable person." After a while the new belief replaces the old one.

Relationships to Self: Identification. You perhaps have heard the story about the elephant and the five blind men. When asked to describe an elephant, the first blind man reached out and felt a leg and said, "Oh, I know what an elephant is like. It's exactly like a tree trunk." The second blind man felt the tail and said, "Oh no, you are wrong. An elephant is exactly like a rope." The third blind man touched an ear and said, "An elephant isn't a tree trunk or a rope, it's like a lotus leaf." The fourth blind man touched the tusk and said, "Oh, my friends, you are mistaken. An elephant is made of bone." And the fifth blind man touched the trunk and said, "Everyone is wrong! I have touched the elephant and it's just like a snake." All the men were right, and yet what they experienced was only a part of the whole. We all have different identities that we take on at different times in life that are only a part of the whole.

Sometimes we identify with our body, and sometimes with our possessions, and sometimes with our families. A man who runs into a burning building to save his jewels is identifying more strongly with his material goods than with his body. One who has lots of cosmetic surgery is often identifying the self with the body.

To begin to loosen the hold your identification has on you, examine it. Who are you? Write down everything that you think and feel you are: For example, Sarah wrote on her list: wife, mother, daughter, artist, cook, lover, and woman. These labels were the major identities that she took on during a day. Identities are not bad; they allow you to function in the world. However, they become difficult when you get lost in the drama and really believe that you are the role, instead of an actor who's playing the role. When you awaken from this illusion, you realize that you're not the role. You are Spirit.

EXERCISE: EXPANDING YOUR DEFINITION OF SELF

Expand your awareness to include everything that you can see from your Vision Quest site. Really imagine that your personal borders extend far beyond your body. Continue to expand your awareness to include the world and the universe and beyond. This is an excellent exercise to expand your definition of self and to begin to lose your sense of self-importance.

Self-importance is actually a limiting definition of self because it defines you as the circumstances of your life. You're actually so much more. When you expand the parameters of your perception, you begin to recognize, in the deepest place within you, the expansive divinity and majesty that dwells within you.

What Is Your Joy?

In your self-assessment, explore what gives you joy in life. What truly makes you happy? What engages you so deeply that you aren't aware of time passing? When do you feel the most content? It's difficult to pursue happiness if you aren't clear what makes you happy. If you're unsure where to begin, start by going back into your childhood and find what gave you joy as a child. Even in the most dysfunctional childhood there are moments of joy. Once you have found the essence of what has given you joy, see if there's a way to bring those same feelings into your present life.

EXERCISE: WHAT GIVES YOU JOY?

List all the times in your life when you truly felt happy. As you look over the list, is there any common theme that runs through all the items? Describe the times, as a child, when you were happiest. Is there a commonality among these experiences of childhood joy?

Where Is Your Power?

Power comes from reaching into your innermost being and finding and living your truth, without question and without hesitation. You glow with inner power when your words come straight from your heart. In life we're encouraged to live according to other people's expectations. We're conditioned to respond to situations based on the way that society dictates we should. However, when you reach into your soul with courage and focus, and interact with the world from that place of truth, you are powerful.

EXERCISE: UNCOVERING YOUR POWER

List all the times in your life when you felt powerful. Is there any common theme that runs through all the items on the list? Describe the times in your childhood when you felt that you were in your power, as well as times when you felt empowered. Is there a commonality among these childhood experiences?

Relationship to Others

Past Relationships. Every person who has been in your life is your teacher and healer. This is true especially of the people with whom you have had the greatest difficulty. The Dalai Lama said that you don't learn tolerance from friends. Every person in your life has allowed you to learn and to grow in compassion and understanding as a human being. Truly, every person you meet is an "assignment from God." In order to step into your future with strength and power, it's very important to heal old emotional wounds and miscommunications with the people who have been in your life. Your Vision Quest is an excellent time to do this because of the energy and clarity that you can garner within yourself. There's a direct correlation between your ability to forgive others and your ability to forgive yourself. Forgiveness can heal.

Several years ago I was giving a seminar in Finland. A downtrodden man who looked as if he had lived a hard life came into the seminar room and sat near the back. At the end of the seminar he came up to talk to me. His mien had completely changed. His deeply lined face was now radiant, and tears streamed down his cheeks. He explained that ten years earlier he had murdered his mother. He had been sent to prison and been released after seven years. He said that although society had forgiven his crime, there wasn't a day, an hour, or even a minute when he had forgiven himself. His life was filled with excruciating guilt. Every day was a living hell. He explained that during one of the seminar exercises, he had "seen" his mother. She came to him softly, radiating love, and said, "Son, you are forgiven. I love you." He instantly felt a deep peace fill him and a heavy burden drop from his shoulders. He said, "I am now ready to live again."

This is the power of forgiveness. Even if you have committed the most heinous act, it does not help you or anyone else to hold on to guilt. Everybody is worthy of redemption. It's important to forgive yourself. If someone has done something harmful to you, forgiveness doesn't necessarily mean that you need to forgive the act. Some acts may be unforgivable. However, forgiving the person, even if you can't forgive the act, can be very beneficial to you.

EXERCISE: PRACTICING FORGIVENESS

As you explore your life, locate those people who have wronged you and the people you have wronged. Who have you been unkind to and who has been unkind to you? Imagine yourself speaking or communicating with each of these individuals and really "speaking your truth." Then listen to them speak their truth to you. Continue this inner dialogue until you reach some kind of resolution or understanding. Review your life and honor all relationships. What haven't you communicated that you need to communicate? If there's someone to whom you haven't expressed your anger, rage, grief, bitterness, or resentment, then imagine yourself doing so now . . . and then listen to what that person has to share with you. Whom do you need to forgive? Forgive him or her. If you just can't do so, then forgive yourself for *not* forgiving others.

Current Relationships

Spend some time exploring your current relationships. Are you satisfied with them? Every person in your life is a reflection of some aspect of you. It's valuable to ascertain what quality within you each person represents. If you have some difficult relationships, the Vision Quest is an excellent place to begin to heal them. Sometimes a remarkable healing of relationships occurs immediately following a Quest.

EXERCISE: IDENTIFY THE SIGNIFICANT PEOPLE IN YOUR LIFE

List the significant people in your life on the left half of a piece of paper. Next to each person's name, write what you feel is his or her most prevalent quality. When you have finished, go down the list of qualities and see how they relate to you. Every person who is significant in your life represents an important aspect of yourself.

Focus on each person who is important in your life. Is there any action that you need to take regarding that person? If there is, make a plan on when and how you're going to implement the change. For example, Joe put his son down as one of his significant relationships. When he looked to see if there was any action he needed to take, he realized that he needed to spend more time with his son. He then decided to take him to a ball game when he returned from his Quest.

If there's something that you need to change in a relationship, be sure to examine how that change will alter every aspect of your life, and make sure you are at peace with that.

Relationship to Your Parents

Your parents (or the people who raised you) have an irrevocable effect on you. Not only did they give you physical birth (if they're your biological parents), but they also gave birth to the early childhood conditioning that most likely continues to color your perception of life. To discover your real self, it's helpful to know what beliefs you acquired from your parents and to ascertain if those beliefs are appropriate to your life now. In addition, it's valuable to discover what your parents stand for and how that relates symbolically to your life. No matter whether they're "good" parents or "bad," they played a valuable role in your spiritual development.

EXERCISE: EXPLORE YOUR RELATIONSHIP TO YOUR PARENTS

How do you feel about your parents? How do you think they feel about you? Do you feel complete with your parents? If not, what do you need in order to feel complete? What do you feel that you didn't get from your parents when you were growing up? Often what you didn't receive emotionally from your parents is what you feel you don't receive from your partner. What you didn't receive from your parents (such as love or trust or tenderness) can also be the gift you have to give to others.

Life Evaluation Questions

If you can't see the patterns in your life, it's difficult to change them. One way to see these patterns is to answer questions intended to reveal the underlying forces at play in your life. Below are questions that you might explore during your Quest. Of course, you don't need to answer them all. They are intended only to highlight some areas of your life that you might want to examine.

Your Relationship with Yourself

- Where are you now in your life physically, emotionally, and spiritually?
- What does the purpose of your life seem to be?
- What have you been putting off in your life?
- What do you need to forgive yourself for?
- What gives you your greatest joy?
- What do you really want to do with your life?
- What is really important to you?
- What have you always dreamed of doing? Why haven't you done it?
- Do you have any habits or addictions or compulsions? Why do you think that you have them?

- Do you have to struggle to get ahead or does life unfold easily for you?

- What are the things that you like best about yourself? What are the things that you dislike about yourself?

- What would you like to change about yourself? Can you accept yourself if you never change?

- Would you like to know exactly when you are going to die? How would your life change if you knew?

- What are you afraid of? What do you need to do to face or release your fears?

Your Relationship to Others

- What don't you want others to know about you?

- What have you never told anyone?

- Are you afraid of anyone?

- Who do you feel closest to?

- What do you think other people think about you?

- When you need help, are you willing to ask for it?

- Who are your people?

- Who are your teachers?

- Can you take compliments without having to explain or demure and say that you don't really deserve it?

- Which public person do you admire (and whom do you dislike) the most and why? (Usually the qualities that you admire or dislike in another are the qualities within yourself that you subconsciously like or dislike.)

- Who is the most important person in your life? Are you happy with the relationship as it is? Is there anything you need to change or heal in this relationship?

Your Relationship to the Divine

- Who, what, and where is the source of your spiritual inspiration?

- What is your name for the Creator?

- Who or what do you think the Creator is?

- What is the purpose of the Creator in your life?

- What do you want the Creator to know about you?

- If you have conditions for the Creator in your life, what are they? Are you willing to let them go?

- What do you think the Creator feels about you?

- Do you think or feel that the Creator has a plan for you? What do you think it is?

- Are you willing to let go completely and allow the Creator to guide your life?

Your Communications

- Do you speak from your heart and say what's on your mind?

- Do you say yes when you mean no, and no when you mean yes?

- Do you say things that you don't really mean just to be polite?

- Do you privately talk negatively about people to whom you are pleasant in person?

- Do you listen when others are talking?

- Do you interrupt others in conversation?

- Do your words match your actions?

Your Relationship to Money

- Are you happy with the abundance you have in your life?

- What are your core beliefs about money?

- Are you afraid of having (or not having) money?

- What would change in your life if you had more money?

- What wouldn't change in your life if you had more money?

- What was your parents' relationship to money?

- Do you believe that you have to work hard to have money?

- What are your judgments about rich people and poor people?

Your Relationship to Sexuality

- Do you enjoy sex? Why or why not?

- Do you prefer the company of your own sex or the opposite sex?

- Are your best friends usually male or female?

- Do you have a recurring sexual fantasy? What would you think of someone else who had that same fantasy?

- What makes you most uncomfortable about sex?

- Is there anything with regard to sex that makes you feel guilty or ashamed?

Your Relationship to Your Career

- What are your skills/gifts? Are you using these skills in your career?

- Are you doing what you *really* want to do with your life?

- Do you enjoy your work?

- What did you really enjoy doing as a child?

- If money weren't an issue, what work would you do?

- What are your career goals?

- Do you keep your commitments?

- Do you do what you say you are going to do? If not, why not?

- Do you take risks in your career?

LIFE SITUATION QUESTIONS

Here are some situation questions to allow you a deeper insight into yourself. These questions don't have "right" or "wrong" answers. Each is aimed at allowing a deeper understanding of yourself. When answering these questions, imagine yourself in the situations and be aware of how you would respond. Probe within yourself to understand why you would respond in a certain way.

As you contemplate these questions, explore your values and see if they came from your own life experience, from your family and friends, or even from past-life experiences. Sometimes the difficulty that arises from trying to answer these questions can bring unresolved conflicts to the surface to be healed. Pay attention to the questions that you don't feel inclined to grapple with. For example, notice if you avoid any question that concerns death. The way you feel about a question can give you as much insight into yourself as the answer itself. Your feelings about the question can also be a sign of concerns within your subconscious mind. Each question has underlying issues that can warrant deep soul searching. Observing the way you deal with these questions on your Vision Quest is an excellent way for you to gain self-understanding.

- If you could live forever in good health would you? Why or why not?

- If you could have five people with you as you were dying, whom would you choose and why?

- If you only had one year to live, what would you do with your time? Would you change anything in your current life? Are you willing to make those changes without imminent death hanging over you? Why or why not?

- If you could have only one of your material possessions, what would it be and why?

- If you could spend the day with anyone in the world, who would it be and why?

- It's late at night and while parking you slightly scratch the side of a new car. No one sees you. Do you leave a note?

- Are you always early, always on time, or always late? How do you feel about people that are always early, on time, or late?

- If you were given one million dollars what would you do with it? Ten million?

- If you could be any animal, what animal would you be? Why?

- If you're in an argument and you realize that you are wrong, do you admit it right away or do you keep defending your point of view.

- If you're walking down the street and find a brown paper bag filled with $10,000 in cash but no identification, would you keep it or hand it in to the police? What if there was someone's name and address in it?

- You are given one million dollars to use for nonpersonal gain. What do you do with it?

- If you could have one perfect day, what would you do from the time you woke up until you went to sleep?

- If you came home from grocery shopping and realized that you had not been charged for an item, would you compensate the grocery store the next time you went? What if you noticed the mistake in the parking lot before you left?

Step 2: Face Your Fears and Release Your Attachments

Face Your Fears

Facing fear takes courage. Most people would rather live their lives within familiar confines than take a step to face the unknown realm where fear dwells. However, illness, weakness, fragmentation, and isolation can result when you live with fear rather than face it, because fear lowers your energy. Facing fear can be terrifying. It can require enormous willpower to step through the veil of illusion that fear emits. And yet facing your fears can be the most empowering thing that you do in your life. Remarkably, you can overcome fears on your Vision Quest through a very simple technique. Simply imagine each fear in its worst possible scenario (even overexaggerate it) and then think of a way either to overcome the situation or to accept the possible outcome. This basic exercise can change the course of your life.

Ray's worst fear was that the Internal Revenue Service would catch him. Before his Quest, when he went through some old tax records, he found a huge mistake in his favor. There was an enormous amount of money on which he hadn't paid taxes. He became obsessively frightened about it. "Should I tell the tax people? What if they find the mistake first? Will I be penalized or even prosecuted?" His fear reached epic proportions. During his Quest he did the exercise where he visualized the worst possible scenario.

He imagined returning home to find that the IRS had confiscated all his possessions, and he was sent to jail. Though of course this is an exaggerated scenario, Ray struggled in his mind until he found a way that he could accept this outcome. He thought, *If I end up in prison, I can teach classes to other prisoners on what I have learned about awareness.* In his visualization he felt good because he was making a difference in so many of the prisoners' lives. When he had finished the exercise, all the fear about his taxes drained out of him and he decided what action to take.

Exercise: Facing Your Fears

"A fear named is a fear tamed." List your fears and confront them.

If you're not sure exactly what you're afraid of, take a moment to visualize yourself in a completely vulnerable situation. This might involve something different for each person. For one it might be physical vulnerability, while for another it might be emotional, intellectual, or perhaps spiritual risk. As you visualize the situation that embodies vulnerability for you, let your mind float freely to see what the worst threat could be. Imagine the worst possible scenario. This is a way to tap into some of your deepest fears.

If you're not sure how to face or confront fear, a simple exercise is to visualize yourself either overcoming your fear or finding a way in which you accept the feared outcome. When you imagine overcoming or accepting a fear, it has less power over you.

Death and Old Age

Your body has a limited time on earth. Your body will die. (You, of course, will not.) There's power in facing the finite nature of the body. Confronting the mortality of your body and facing your death with courage and compassion can allow you to live life more fully. Until you accept your death, it's difficult to truly live. Native Americans have an expression: "Today is a good day to die," which can be interpreted as "I am complete in this moment. I am ready. I am enough."

We live in a culture that reveres youth and beauty and denigrates old age and illness. However, all life's stages have value and beauty, even the pain, suffering, and ignobility of old age. I want to experience life in all its richness. Even my tirade against the indignities of age is precious to me. It's all part of the earth plane experience, and I want to feel it all while I'm here.

EXERCISE: FACING DEATH

Imagine going forward to your time of death. Fully confront your death with courage and grace. Grieve if you need to. You cannot truly live until you are willing to face your death.

Release Your Attachments

I lived in a Zen monastery for over two years, during which time I developed a deep appreciation for Zen stories. This is one of my favorites: Two Zen monks were walking when they came to a river. On the riverbank was a very beautiful young woman who was afraid to cross the river. She asked for help. One of the monks stepped forward, hefted her onto his back, and carried her across the river. He gently put her down on the other side, and continued to walk.

An hour later, the other monk, unable to hold back any longer, burst out, "How could you dare to carry a woman on your back? You are a monk and a renunciate!"

To which the first monk gently smiled and replied, "Oh, are you still carrying her? I released her when I put her down on the shore."

What are you carrying around with you? What are you attached to? Are you attached to your perpetual anger? Are you holding on to an addiction? Are you unduly attached to your possessions? Are you overly cleaving to your children? Are you attached to your beliefs and point of view? Your attachments define and confine you. They can limit the way you experience the world around you.

Some people think that tenaciously holding on to an attachment or point of view is what defines a strong person; however, sometimes it's letting go that makes one strong. The opposite of attachment is surrender, which doesn't necessarily mean that you give up anything or deny your true feelings. In fact, when you release your attachment to another person, often the relationship deepens because it's not based on need. Attachment lessens you, while nonattachment catapults you toward your potential. Surrendering means shifting your perspective to accept yourself and your life in its totality in the moment. It's a natural state of grace.

EXERCISE: LEARN TO LET GO

Identify the attachments in your life. Close your eyes. Relax, and imagine that there are invisible cords of energy flowing between you and each object of your attachment. Visualize releasing or cutting the cords that bind you to your attachment. Feel the cords drop away.

Step 3. Tap Into the Spirit Power Within You

Shape-Shifting

There's an energy field that surrounds and penetrates us. It imparts life to all living things. It binds the universe together. During your Quest you can gain awareness of this majestic life force. This is exciting because you begin to see that life is not always as it seems. You can gain an awareness of the awesome and powerful dimensions that lie within you.

You were born into a collective thought form that defines reality in a particular way. Our collective reality agrees that all form is solid and that time is linear. In recent times, scientists have begun to refute these time-honored assumptions. Despite this new information, our shared collective reality still defines time as staid and form as solid. However, native cultures throughout the world perceive reality in a very different light. Native wisdom declares that everything, including solid objects, is made of energy in different forms. Shamans throughout history have understood the flexible nature of time and have been able to stretch, condense, and even loop time back on itself. In your Quest you can step out of the collective reality and thus out of your personal probability pattern. When you see the world through new eyes, you begin to be the master of your destiny.

The way to begin to see the world through new eyes is to learn to shape-shift. To shape-shift means to expand your awareness so that you can enter the consciousness of other life forms. It also means to shift your personal parameters so that you can sense the energy fields around you. When you've seen the world through the eyes of a butterfly, life expands majestically and nothing looks the same. From the perception of a butterfly, the world is filled with vibrations, colors, and shapes that seem unrecognizable and indefinable at first; in fact, there's no perception of human beings in a butterfly's reality, aside from movement and color. A butterfly perceives an entirely different reality from ours. How do I know this? I've looked at the world through the eyes of a butterfly.

My teacher, Dancing Feather, a Pueblo Native American, was the most humble and sincere person I ever knew. He didn't speak much, but when he did, he spoke the truth. He told me that he was in the Fox family. I asked what that meant. He said that he, his father, his grandfather, and all of his ancestors turned themselves into foxes to gain wisdom and knowledge of the inner realms. I replied, "Oh, you mean that you imagined that you were foxes?" He looked at me with such patient eyes and said softly, "No, Denise. We really turn ourselves into foxes." In that moment I felt truth resonate through his words. Even though it's hard for me to comprehend a human turning into a fox, I knew that Dancing Feather always spoke the truth.

When you begin to shape-shift, you realize that all permutations of life reside within you. This makes a powerful stand for environmentalism because you begin to realize: "I don't just live on the earth; I am the earth." When you experience yourself as the earth and the mountains and trees and birds, you develop a passion for contributing to the environment.

EXERCISE: SHAPE-SHIFTING

Learning to shape-shift can allow you to step out of your probability pattern and can open an entirely new dimension to your life. As you sit in your sacred circle on your Quest, look at the environment around you and imagine yourself dissolving and then reforming as a tree, a rock, a cloud, a beetle, a flower, or whatever is in your immediate environment. Notice how this feels.

To acclimate yourself to shape-shifting, visualize molding your body. To do this, close your eyes, relax, and imagine that you're stepping out of your body. Turn around and see your body in front of you. Reach out with your spirit energy hands and mold the body like clay in a potter's hands. You can either reform the shape of the body or you can mold your body into another form, such as a stone or an eagle.

Judy Knight, of Great Britain, reported the following:

I shape-shifted with a seal who was in the bay most of the time. I shape-shifted with the birds and with the sea otters. They chattered as they swam past. I shape-shifted with the trees, the spiders, the cloud people, and the stars. I had wanted to see a raccoon. One morning I was sitting waiting for the sun to rise and at the water's edge was a raccoon. Every wish was granted. I was blissful and happy.

Sensing Energy

We're immersed in an ocean of energy. The energy that is around us flows and moves in constant, ever-changing currents through time and space. Beneath the surface of fixed objects, which exist in a linear river of time, is the reality that energy swirls into form, and coalesces once again. The world around us and within us is an interplay of these patterns of energy in ever-fluid relationship. Underlying this motion is a cosmic order.

When you begin to develop the ability to sense energy, you will discover that all matter has color and sound. Every plant emanates a shimmering radiant light and at the same time emits a soft hum unique to its species. Every blade of grass, every flower, tree, animal, bird, and even every stone emits light and has a unique sound. Some sounds are like low drones and some are like finely tuned hums, and others are even somewhat lyrical. To step into the realm of energy, shape-shift into another form and expand your awareness into the realm of light and sound. For example, if you shape-shift into a dandelion, imagine what sound and colors the plant might emit. Immerse yourself in this awareness. Become the light and sound of the dandelion.

EXERCISE: SENSING ENERGY

Relax, close your eyes, and imagine that you're in a sacred meadow. Imagine that your awareness expands so that you can sense, see, and smell the subtle vibrations within the meadow. Then imagine that you are moving your hand in front of you, until you can see a trail of light and hear a sound in your hand's wake as you move it back and forth. You can perceive the ripples of energy flowing through and around it.

Sacred Drumming

One of the fastest ways to tap into your Spirit power is to drum. From ancient times to the present, people all over the world have incorporated the drum into their cultures. The drum has the ability to alter consciousness and thus has been used for a variety of purposes, from rousing warriors to accomplish remarkable feats, to being used for healing purposes, to inner mystic voyages. The sound of the drum literally alters brain waves. This has been verified in scientific research. Native Americans call the drum the "canoe" or the "horse" because of its ability to allow one to travel to spiritual realms.

Your drum can intensify whatever intention you have for your Vision Quest. For instance, if your intention is to send healing to your family, your drumming can magnify that intention in a powerful way. If you want to travel inward and explore deep aspects of yourself, playing the drum close to your heart can alter your consciousness so that you are transported deeply into the inner realms.

On the Quests that I lead, we make drums beforehand and many take their drums into their sacred circles. If you drum while on your Quest, it has the potential to tap you into your intuition and even connect you to the rhythms of the cosmos. If you decide to take a drum with you, make sure that your drumming won't attract attention, as it can disturb your Vision Quest if people gather to hear you drum. If your spot is close to other people, you can tap quietly on the drum with your hand or fingers, which makes little noise but can still help you to travel into inner realms.

Exercise: Sacred Drumming

Hold your drum close to your chest and allow your awareness to fill the interior of the drum. Rub your hand in a circle around the outer area of the drum to connect more deeply with it. Begin drumming with a double beat.

This is an excellent way to start because the two-beat rhythm connects you to the heartbeat, which is the most primordial sound for human beings.

After feeling this sound resonate inside you, use whatever beat feels best to you, simply allowing a natural rhythm to evolve. When you stop drumming, close your eyes and focus your awareness on the inner realm within you. This can produce profound results.

Find Your Spirit Name

There's power in your name, and it's part of your Spirit power. Your name is much more than the label that people call you; it's your unique energy pattern vibration. Used properly, it can open you to spiritual realms and heightened consciousness. It can also be a catalyst for growth, for your name is a direct link to your soul. When you know the name of something or someone, there's a connection between you and that object or person. In ancient metaphysical traditions, people were careful whom they told their true name to because it was believed that if someone knew your name they could have power over you.

The words we use to describe objects and people have a powerful effect. Companies pay thousands of dollars to come up with names for products that inspire or entice. For example, car names like Bronco and Mustang inspire a rough-and-ready adventurous individual. Research has shown that a person's name can dramatically affect their personality and the way that others relate to them. But in a much deeper sense, our name defines how we see and feel about ourselves.

In native cultures, one had a birth name and then at the time of ascent into adulthood, there was a naming ceremony. During the ceremony a name was given that not only was a reflection of the spirit of the person but was intended to imbue power into the individual. For example, a child named Eagle Bear would have a definition of self that radiated strength and power. In present times, actors often change their names to give a perception of something grand and exciting, and frequently career changes follow. In our society we do not have a tradition of names of merit. We only have a tradition of birth names, which usually don't reflect our inner spirit.

There's value in discovering a spirit name on your Quest that reflects who you are now and also strengthens the path of who you are to become in the future. Your spiritual name may come from observing nature and the environment around you. Raven Heart gained her name when she saw a noble-looking raven as she sat in her sacred circle. She said that she felt a deep sense of empathy and communion with the bird and knew that Raven was a part of her true name. Your name may also come in the form of a word or words that don't have meaning in English yet have a profound feeling associated with them because of the sound vibration. Ashara's name came to her during a dream while she was on a pilgrimage. She knew it was her true name as soon as she heard it. She said she felt a warm tide of energy surge through her every time she thought of it, even though she had never heard the name before. Your spirit name can also refer to qualities that define your personal attributes, such as the name Strong Heart or Spirit Singer.

The meaning of your spiritual name may unfold for you long after you receive it. Martin searched for his name on his Quest and his attention was drawn to a broken tree that had fallen down. He thought, *Broken Tree—that can't be my name. It doesn't sound very spiritual.* But his inner voice kept whispering the name to him, *Broken Tree. Broken Tree.* He said, "Well, Broken Tree it is." In the months following his Quest, he began to think about his name. In his mind's eye he saw an image of a tree that had broken and fallen across a deep chasm. As he looked he saw that people were able to cross the chasm because of the strength and steadiness of the broken tree. As he reflected on his life he saw that even though he had been broken (he was a recovering alcoholic), through his "brokenness" he was able to help and have compassion for others. In addition to his work as an attorney, he volunteered in the prison system to help convicts overcome their addictions. When he had this realization, he saw that there was great power and beauty in the name Broken Tree.

When you discover your true name you may choose to keep it secret or to reveal it only to those close to you, or you may choose to use your name publicly. Either way your spirit name can contribute to your personal power.

EXERCISE: FINDING YOUR SPIRIT NAME

Relax and breathe deeply and fully. Open heart, mind, and soul and ask that the Creator send you a name that reflects your spirit. Be open to whatever form your name appears in. Sometimes you have to try your name out for a while to see if it feels right. To do this, keep repeating your new name aloud over and over again. Notice how the sound of your name makes you feel. If it's the right name for you, you will feel stronger just by saying it.

Find Your Spirit Animal

The use of spirit animals (called totems, animal allies, or power animals) throughout history is well documented. Native peoples throughout the world understand the value of connecting with one's power animal. In addition, in some European mystic traditions, spirit animals are considered important allies to help attune to inner strengths. For example, someone working with the fox spirit (called "fox medicine" in the Native American culture) can develop the ability to become "invisible" when needed. They can enter and leave a room without being noticed if they choose. Someone working with "bear medicine" can develop inner strength. There's great value in determining and attuning to your totem animal. In fact, for many people, the discovery of their spirit animal is their single most important experience in their Vision Quest. Connecting to your totem animal not only further deepens your connection to the earth and the creatures of our beautiful planet, but it begins to bring into your life the qualities that are associated with the animal.

As part of your Quest you may want to discover what your animal totems are. Sometimes your spirit animals will appear in your dreams, sometimes an intuitive awareness begins to dawn within you, and sometimes they will physically visit you during your Quest.

Catherine, a warm, easygoing woman from Middlesex, England, came to the Vision Quest not because there was a major issue in her life that needed to be resolved, but because she wanted to spend some time away from the pressures of everyday life to deepen her connection to the Creator:

As the start of the Vision Quest approached, everybody . . . seemed to get a bit jittery. I began to wonder whether I could spend three days on my own out in the open. I suppose my biggest concern was whether I could go for so long without food. Would I start eating the grass by the end of the first day? Then as we all sat in the Longhouse [a large communal Native American meeting space] on the last evening before the Vision Quest talking about how we felt, a sense of peace and contentment flooded through me. I felt totally resolute and ready for the start.

[On the day of the Vision Quest I was intuitively] guided to a beautiful place. There were trees on three sides, but straight ahead . . . looked out over the water to the other islands. It was very calm and peaceful. I spent some time watching a sailboat glide silently out of the gentle mist. A gull floated by very slowly on a piece of jetsam. I felt an overwhelming sense of acceptance by Great Spirit. I came to know deep in my heart that I am part of the great web of life, that what I do is of value and makes a difference.

Toward the end of the first day I heard a strange knocking sound in the tree about my sacred circle. It was a woodpecker; the first time I had even seen one! [I felt that] the woodpecker was one of my power animals, not by my choice but because a friend had told me that the woodpecker is the power animal for my birth sign. When I first heard this news I felt disappointed. I would have preferred the mighty eagle rather than the lowly woodpecker, but with time I came to love and accept the woodpecker as my power animal. Woodpeckers drum [with their beaks on trees] mainly to get at their food, but sometimes they drum for the sheer love of it. I love to drum, too. It was through hearing the sound of the drum that Great Spirit first called me to the Native American path.

The woodpecker above my sacred circle continued to drum away for ages. From time to time the lichen that he was pecking from the branches showered down onto me. A true blessing from Great Spirit. Finally the woodpecker flew away, but when I woke up the next morning the first sound I heard was the woodpecker again. This time he did not stay long but he had come to make sure everything was all right. I felt looked after by Great Spirit. The spirit of the woodpecker stays with me always. I have painted the drum I made on the island with a woodpecker design so we always drum together. It helps me to connect back to my sacred circle and the sense of oneness with Great Spirit I felt there.

When I got back to London I felt jet-lagged and I was thrown straight away into the hurly-burly of life and work in the big city. It was as if I had suddenly lost everything I had felt on the island. Slowly the connection with Great Spirit got stronger and deeper again. It endures and has become an essential part of me and my daily life. It always helps in times of stress or uncertainty to connect back to my sacred circle on the island and the deep sense of belonging I felt there.

Patricia Dawson, from Great Britain, wrote to tell me how she discovered her totem on her Quest:

I was so tired; my life at present is so physically and mentally exhausting that as I lay in my circle I just wanted to sleep. I felt myself relaxing quickly and sleep was close but I was immediately aware of a smallish bear curling up against my back and melting into me. It was actually physically impossible as

*my back was resting against the hill. I felt no fear and felt no
need to turn to look at it. I remember thinking, "Oh yes, good,
it's a bear." Then I fell asleep.*

EXERCISE: FINDING YOUR SPIRIT ANIMAL

Relax and breathe deeply and fully. Open your heart,
mind, and soul and ask that your animal spirit come to
you. Imagine that you're in a beautiful place in nature.
Make it seem as real as you can. Imagine that a dense fog
descends on the land. Be aware that your spirit animal is
coming to you through the mists. Imagine reaching your
hand out into the mists and touching your totem. Notice
whether you feel fur, hair, feathers, reptilian skin, scales,
a shell, a hide, or something else. Use your intuition to be
aware of what kind of animal you are touching. Gradually
the mist rises; imagine talking to your animal ally.

The meanings of your totems are very individual. The specific meanings of spirit animals change from culture to culture
and from person to person. The meaning of a spirit animal will
also vary according to the associations the animal has for that
person. For example, if a child had a large German shepherd that
acted as a protective guardian, a dog totem might represent protection, loyalty, and safety. If another child had a small, lively dog,
"dog medicine" might represent the qualities of joyfulness and
play. I find that one of the best ways to discover the meaning of
your power animal is to study its habits in nature. For example, in
nature, bears are creatures of habit. They will often go to the same
apple grove at the same time every day and use the same winter
den every year. Hence, people who work with "bear medicine" are
often creatures of habit. There's no totem that is better than any
other totem; each has its own power and beauty.

Here are some ways to discover the meaning of your spirit animal after you return from your Quest:

- Go on a journey in your imagination and visualize your totem in its natural habitat. Imagine that your totem can talk and ask it what its meaning is in your life.

- Research your totem in nature books. Find out what particular behavior it has in its environment.

- Imagine yourself becoming your spirit animal and notice what qualities *you* feel.

- Research your heritage and find out the meaning your totem animal may have had for your ancestors.

- Research your past lives. The meaning of your totem may come from a reincarnation memory. For example, in the Orient, the crane is connected to longevity, but in Celtic mythology the crane is sacred to the ruler of the underworld and is the harbinger of death.

The following lists provide a condensed introduction to the meanings of totems and are by no means a definitive guide, for the realm of totems is both vast and diverse. An in-depth recounting of the qualities and special medicine power of each animal would fill several books.

LAND ANIMALS

Antelope: Swiftness, speed, agility
Ape/monkey: Protection, family, ingenuity
Ass/donkey: Surefootedness, determination
Badger: Ferocity, courage, tenacity, boldness
Bear: Healer, strength, stamina, introspection

Beaver: Persistence, group harmony, productivity

Bison/buffalo: Abundance, courage, determination

Bull: Strength, stubbornness, determination, power, fecundity

Cat: Independence, cleverness, mystery

Cougar/mountain lion: Silent power, self-confidence

Cow: Fertility, contentment

Coyote: Cleverness, playful, family orientation

Deer/stag: Grace, fertility, regeneration, strength

Dog: Loyalty, protection, faithfulness

Elephant: Patience, royalty, power

Elk: Stamina, nobility, warrior spirit

Fox: Camouflage, cunning, quickness

Giraffe: Farsightedness, reaching goals

Goat: Surefootedness, reaching new heights

Hippopotamus: Birth, Great Mother

Horse: Power, freedom, grace

Leopard/panther: Valor, elusiveness, hidden knowledge

Lion: Self-confidence, radiant power

Moose: Balance, gentle yet strong, majestic yet awkward

Mouse: Discovery, attention to detail, invisibility, scrutiny

Opossum: Strategy, stillness

Otter: Joy, playfulness, receptivity

Panther/leopard: Intuition, inner power

Pig/boar/sow: Courage, cunning

Rabbit/hare: Fertility, intuition, quick thinking

Raccoon: Adaptation, creativity, dexterity

Ram/sheep: Balance in precarious situations

Rat: Cunning, assertiveness, intelligence

Rhinoceros: Ancient wisdom

Skunk: Self-respect, self-confidence, courage

Squirrel: Energy, intelligence, discovery

Weasel: Stealth, cunning

Wolf: Family, loyalty, strength

AQUATIC ANIMALS

Dolphin: Joy, peace, sacred messenger, wisdom

Eel: Grace, power

Octopus: Ancient wisdom

Salmon: Spiritual knowledge, determination

Seal: Grace, joy

Tuna: Ancient power, strength, mobility

Whale: Trust, faith, balance, harmony

WINGED CREATURES

Bat: Transformation, primordial darkness, rebirth, initiation

Blackbird: Ancient wisdom, inner knowledge, mysticism, hidden insights

Bluebird: Joy, confidence, gentleness, modesty, contentedness

Blue Jay: Courage, speaking one's truth, adaptability

Canary: Sacred sounds, sensitivity, opening of throat chakra

Cardinal: Confidence, vitality

Chickadee/titmouse: Cheerfulness, joy, endurance, fearlessness

Chicken: Service, sacrifice, fertility

Cock/rooster: Sexuality, alertness, fertility, enthusiasm

Crane: Longevity, focus, discipline, vigilance

Crow: Magic, mystery, great intelligence, messenger from realm of Spirit

Dove/pigeon: Peace, feminine energies, maternal instincts, gentleness, love

Duck: Emotional balance, domestic harmony

Eagle: Illumination, Spirit power, creation

Falcon/kestrel: Speed, grace, power, absolute determination to reach a goal

Goose: Sacred quests, transformation, mystical journeys, community

Hawk: Visionary, strength, messenger from Spirit, decisiveness

Heron: Dignity, self-reliance, individuality, patience

Hummingbird: Joy, tireless energy, delight, hope

Kingfisher: Peace, prosperity, love, luck

Ostrich: Groundedness, balance between ancient wisdom and practicality

Owl: Wisdom, visionary, magic, feminine energies, ancient secrets

Parrot: Optimism, joy, confidence

Peacock: Magnificence, sacred protection, dignity, self-confidence

Pelican: Generosity, self-sacrifice, buoyancy, prosperity

Raven: Messenger from Sprit, ancient mysteries, shape-shifting

Robin: New beginnings, joy, activation of creative inner force, happiness

Seagull: Emotional balance, communication, spiritual messengers

Sparrow/wren: Cheerfulness, love of home, fertility, boldness

Stork: Fertility, balanced home, new beginnings

Swallow: Daring, freedom, grace

Swan: Transformation, intuition, grace, higher wisdom, inner beauty

Turkey: Blessings, generosity, service

Vulture: Death and rebirth, prophecy, Great Mother

Woodpecker: Industrious, focus, sacred rhythms

AMPHIBIANS AND REPTILES

Chameleon: Adaptation, willingness to change, art of invisibility, sensitivity

Cobra: Royalty, power, wisdom

Crocodile/alligator: Ancient power, initiation

Frog: Transformation, purification, new beginnings

Lizard: Guardian of the dreamtime, divination

Snake: Wisdom, initiation, transformation, creativity, healing

Toad: Prosperity, abundance, Spirit of Earth

Turtle/tortoise: Longevity, stability, home, Mother Earth

SPIDERS AND INSECTS

Ant: Industriousness, stamina, community

Bee: Fertility, abundance, concentration, love

Beetle/scarab: Metamorphosis, creation, resurrection

Butterfly: Transformation, transmutation, joy, beauty

Dragonfly: Dream messenger, joy, light

Spider: Creativity, fate

MYTHICAL CREATURES

Centaur: Mystical masculine power

Dragon: Immense spiritual power, protection

Griffin (half-lion/half-eagle): Connection between heaven and earth

Pegasus: Spiritual inspiration, grace, holiness

Phoenix: Transformation, rebirth, new beginnings

Satyr (half-man/half-goat): Nature spirit, music, dancing, joy

Sphinx (half-human/half-lion): Initiation, Dark Mother

Unicorn: Love, gentleness, strength, purity

Find Your Spirit Song

Often on a Vision Quest a personal power song emerges. This is a song that springs forth from your soul. It's not necessarily a song that others will enjoy or that will make the top ten on the charts. It's a song that carries your power, communicating from your soul and resonating straight from dreams or visions, yet sometimes you have to experiment with the words and the melody. Some power songs are a single phrase repeated over and over again (such as, "I am one with the Infinite Sun"), but they can also be a ballad that tells your story, hopes, dreams, and visions.

Your song can also come in the form of chanting or toning. A chant can be a sound or sounds that are repeated again and again (such as, *hey ya, hey ya*) or it can be the repetition of a word that has power for you (such as, *loving*). If you find yourself using a word that is special to you (*joy*, for instance) when you chant, completely immerse yourself in the meaning as well as the sound of the word. When you do this you are actually bringing the power of that word into your life and into the world at large. Sound is vibration, and the world around us is made of vibration. As you chant, merge with your sound and follow the sound into your environment. Notice how the vibration of sound affects the world around you.

When you are chanting, your inhalation connects you to Mother Earth. Your exhalation connects you to Father Sky. Your breath aligns the two opposing yet harmonious forces in the universe: male and female, or dark and light, or inward and outward. When the two forces are in harmony, the planet is in harmony. As you chant, you are bringing these forces into harmony within you and through you to the universe.

Exercises: Quest Songs

Chant your name (either your birth name or your spirit name) over and over again. Ancient mystery schools understood the power of the word. Your name is an energy pattern that connects you to your soul. Repetitive chanting of your name unleashes your soul's potential.

Imagine that you're singing the world into existence. Be creative. Use any sounds that seem to match whatever you are singing.

Sing your prayers. Create a healing song. Sing a song for healing of others. Sing your soul into the universe.

Find Your Spirit Dance

Sacred dance is prayer in motion. In your sacred circle during your Quest, allow your body to express your feelings through movement. This can contribute to an integration of mind and body. When children feel an emotion, they express it fully, both emotionally and physically. Often there will be rhythmic movement at the same time as the emotion is expressed. Children can pound on the floor in anger one minute and then jump up and down with glee a minute later. The reason why children can move rapidly from one emotion to another is that they allow emotions and feelings to flow through them. If you feel angry, dance your anger. Allowing your body to express exactly what you're feeling will allow you to move through your anger more quickly.

As adults we're programmed not to show our emotions; we're certainly not expected to express our emotions through movement and dance. So if, in the beginning, it feels strange to stand up in your medicine wheel and start dancing, then start by just swaying back and forth until you get used to the feeling of movement. Let your swaying express what you feel. One way to get your emotions to flow through you is to move your body. After you get comfortable with swaying, begin to move your arms, head, and legs. Dance your sadness, your sorrow, and your pain. Dance your joy. Celebrate your life through dance. Each of us has a unique vibration and rhythm. Your personal rhythm is a sonorous, deep, and constant rhythm that defines the essence of you. Of course, your surface rhythms change and flow all the time, but your inner rhythm remains the same. When you organize your life in harmony with your personal rhythm, life unfolds magically and powerfully. When you're out of harmony with your personal rhythm, there's disharmony in your life.

EXERCISE: SPIRIT DANCE

Move deep into yourself and imagine that you have found the rhythm of your true essence. Dance that essence. Dance your totem. Dance the environment around you. Dance the earth. Dance the clouds. Dance your past, your present, and your future. Dance until instead of being the dancer, you become the dance. Dissolve yourself until the only thing that exists is the dance. Become the movement of the stars in the heavens. Become the rhythm and harmony of the cosmos. Dance through the universe. Dance with abandon and joy . . . and then you will be free.

Several years ago during a Vision Quest I was leading, I climbed up a ridge to check on someone. As I quietly stepped up to a steep precipice, I was privileged to witness something extraordinary and wondrous. I watched from a distance as a strong and hearty Norwegian man completely dissolved himself into dance. To use words for what I saw and felt doesn't begin to describe the magic of the moment. There was something primordial and powerful in his dance. The movements seemed to transcend time, and I felt that I was seeing some primitive and powerful ritual that gave fertility to the land and a fecund spirit to the people.

As he danced, I felt that the doors to life were opening and that the land he danced on was made holy and sacred through his movements. I sensed a great gathering of spiritual elders surrounding him as he danced in his hallowed circle. I quietly slipped away, feeling that I had seen a great wonder. Later, after the Quest, I talked to him about his dancing. He said that he had danced for hours, without stopping to rest, through the night and day, but had felt no fatigue. I believe his dance allowed him to transcend time and space to enter another dimension where he tapped into his Spirit power.

Prayer Sticks

Ceremony and ritual have long been part of the human condition because they allow us to focus our thoughts, dreams, and desires into a conscious form. The inner psyche can pour forth through them, and they are a catalyst to bring desire into form. Creating a prayer stick on your Vision Quest can add clarity to your vision and can even change the course of your life. A prayer stick gives tangible form to your prayers. It's an ornamented power object that is created with ceremony and intention. Sometimes the stick is decorated with moss and feathers and shells, sometimes with beads and leather and precious stones, and sometimes colored yarn is wrapped around it. It's not the method of creation that is important. It's the spirit with which it's made that imbues it with energy. There's great power in the act of creating a prayer stick. You can use prayer sticks on your Quest for your personal prayers, to chronicle your life, and to help change your life.

Prayer sticks were originally used by the Plains Indians for prayers for a hunt, for rain, for planting, or for a loved one. The tribe's survival depended on nature, and prayer sticks were thought to be an essential part of aligning with the mysterious forces of Great Spirit. They were originally made in several ways, according to the focus on the prayers, and varied in size and decoration. For example, a prayer stick for an abundant harvest was made by painting two sticks green with black tips, and tying them together with cording of a specific length. One stick symbolized the male force and the other the female force. Usually the female stick was given a face. A small corn husk bundle containing cornmeal, seeds, pollen, and honey was tied to the sticks. Connected to the bundle were turkey feathers and herbs. Usually every prayer stick contained a turkey feather because turkey was considered the "giveaway" bird, meaning that turkeys sacrifice themselves for the good of all beings, and the feather acted as a reminder that everything you do should be for the good of all beings. The use of prayer sticks has evolved over the years, and they are now used in many different ways.

Find Your Prayer Stick

The entire process of creating your stick is sacred. It begins with the discovery of your stick before your Quest. To find a stick, go into nature, still your mind, and clearly state your intention. You are putting out the "call" for your stick. Trance Walk to find your stick. (See the previous chapter for information about trance walking.) You'll know it's the right stick because there will be something different and special about it. There's great variety in the sticks that are used: small, large, twisted, straight, thick, and thin. Some people have used very small twigs and some have used huge sticks that can be classified only as small logs. Once you have found your stick, Trance Walk to find objects with which you want to decorate it, such a pinecones, moss, grasses, shells, feathers, leaves, or twigs. You can also use colored string or yarn, beads, paint, pieces of leather, or strips of fabric.

Use Your Prayer Stick for Personal Prayers

To create a prayer stick for your prayers, first be very clear about what you are praying for. This is essential. Marlin wanted physical healing. His arthritis was causing him concern. He chose a very healthy green flexible stick. He told me he didn't want a stick that was brittle because that was how the arthritis in his body felt. On the second day of his Quest, he began the creation of his prayer stick by holding it in front of himself and saying, "I dedicate you to excellent health and flexibility in my body and in my life." Continuing to hold his intention clearly in his mind, he used spring-green moss and sky-blue yarn to make an intricate decoration on his stick. He wanted his prayer stick to radiate a feeling of good health and strength. It took many hours to complete. When he looked at his completed prayer stick, he said he felt stronger than he had for a long time.

You can also make a prayer stick to send prayers to another person or even to a world situation or to an ideal. For example, you can make a prayer stick dedicated to all the people of the planet. (As a suggestion, pray only for the highest good and don't infringe on others. In other words, as an example, don't pray that everyone in your office stops smoking. Instead pray that you breathe only fresh, clean air. You never know, you might get a promotion into an office in which no one smokes.) As you wind the yarn around and around your stick, imagine you are weaving a spirit of love into the world around you.

When you've completed your prayer stick, put it out overnight in a place where the morning sun will touch it. It's said that when the first morning light touches your stick, your prayers go to the Creator.

Use Your Prayer Stick for Your Life

You can use your prayer stick as a symbolic representation of your life. To do this, designate one end of the stick as the time of your birth and the beginning of life. Put something on that spot on the stick that symbolizes how you view your birth into this life. Then, as you work up the stick, mark the major events in your life with different objects. Once you have completed the stick, look at it and see if you feel good about it and it seems an accurate symbolic representation of your life. Rework it until you feel that it conveys your life. If there's anything in your life that you are unhappy about, try reweaving and reworking that aspect of your life where it appears on your stick. Circling the string around and around is like reweaving the soul.

Gregory, a businessman from New Zealand, had a very dramatic experience at one of my Vision Quests that he felt was helped by his prayer stick. He had come to the Quest to try to heal his very strained relationships with his wife and his two daughters. He decided to create a prayer stick to help improve that aspect of his life. As he decorated his stick he put a black bead on it for him, a red bead for his wife, and two yellow beads for his girls. When he had finished, he looked at it and saw that he had placed his black bead a substantial distance from his family beads. He took off the decorations and rewove the stick, but this time with the beads closer. When he looked at it, it still didn't seem right. All afternoon and into the evening he worked on his prayer stick until he finally felt a sense of union with his family. Curiously, at the very time that he was reworking his prayer stick, his wife and daughters were discussing the family relationships. They concluded their discussion feeling a great deal of understanding for Gregory. He said that when he returned home from the Quest, it was as if a miracle had occurred—instead of strife and discord, there was a wonderful sense of love and community in his family. Gregory felt that he had literally changed his life through the creation of his prayer stick.

Merita Käänta, a journalist from Sweden, found that the creation of her stick on her Quest helped her unite opposing aspects of herself:

> I started making my prayer stick. I had found a small branch with a lump in the bottom that split into two at the end. The lump on my stick represented Mother Earth and the split limb branch represented me in constant battle with myself. I felt [that the split represented the split between my ego and my spirit. It also represented the split between my present and my past.] I decided to weave together my ego and spirit, also my present and my past. So this was what I did. I wove these two

parts together with yarn, building a bridge between the two op-posing aspects of myself.

Sometimes the creation of a prayer stick can be a catalyst for change, as it was for Isja Feenstra, a therapist from the Netherlands:

> *As soon as I had made my prayer stick, which was a beauti-ful process, full of learning, I felt myself sliding away. Old stuff, old grief came up. More and more I felt abandoned, and alone. I became sick and cold and cried. At the end, I knew the source of my main grief and longing. Then Paulina [one of the Quest assistants] came. I allowed her into my circle. I felt nothing. She held me in her arms, and consoled me softly. Very slowly I could allow the warmth of a human touch to fill me. I calmed down, left my circle, and greeted a little spider. I had the feeling that a part of my ego had died. It took time to recover, but I felt calm, peaceful, and loved by the others who surrounded me.*

When your Quest is complete, you can take your prayer stick home with you as a reminder of your Quest or you can burn it cer-emoniously. In some traditions it's left in nature; however, do this only if everything on your stick is organic and can decompose easily.

Step 4. Give Thanks

Thankfulness helps you to be receptive to the life force of the universe. If you don't express your gratitude, you lessen your life force. Being appreciative empowers and strengthens you. When you call for a vision with gratefulness flowing through your heart, assistance from the spiritual realm floods into your being. This is a universal law. If you have been praying for help and guidance and no one seems to be listening, start being thankful. Let go of your prayers for what you want and immerse yourself in thankfulness for what you have. This is an act of power. Even if, in the beginning, you have trouble being thankful, act as if you are thankful. There most certainly are things in your life for which you are appreciative. Focus your awareness on those things. It's essential to be in a state of gratitude for wisdom received, for this is the mystic path to inner truth. When you are thankful, it's inevitable that you will gain in wisdom and inner strength.

An old woman once told me that in Native American tradition, one never prayed in order to receive something; one prayed only to give thanks. She said that this concept was central to understanding Native American medicine. This is a valuable concept. When you focus on what is already good about your life, feelings of neediness and of not being good enough tend to fade away into the background. Their urgency seems suddenly less important. Being grateful for what you already have attracts even more good into your life.

Give Thanks for Your Life

If you hold your life in the context of misery and suffering, life becomes a string of difficult events to overcome, but if you hold your life in the context of gratefulness, every experience you have is a gift and offers great value. On your Quest, mentally go through the events in your life and at each milestone stop and allow a feeling of thankfulness to embrace the entire event. Mary did this on her Vision Quest. She had had a difficult life. Her father had abandoned the family when she was seven years old and her mother had become an alcoholic. Often Mary had to take care of her younger brother and sister when her mother was drunk. Mary had been in therapy and had worked through many of the deep issues that had arisen from her childhood, but she still held on to a feeling of deep despair about her traumatic past.

On her Vision Quest, instead of feeling resentful and bitter, Mary began to feel thankful for the experiences in her life. She said that usually when she thought of her overall life she felt a sense of sadness fill her. But on her Quest she tried going through her life with the spirit of appreciation. Even though it was hard, as she went through every experience she tried to find something that was good about it. She came to see that the events of her life were not without purpose. Every event had a hidden gift for her. Instead of feeling the usual resentment about having to take care of her siblings, she allowed herself to feel thankful for those experiences. When she did this, she saw that those experiences allowed her to develop a caring attitude for those less fortunate. (Mary is a highly valued nurse who works in hospices.) She said that it was such an amazing experience to feel grateful for events that she had resented all her life.

Each of the experiences in your life has been important and valuable and has allowed you to become who you are. When you review your life feeling thankful, you can begin to transform the way that you see your past and can influence your future. There's great power in this, for the spirit of thankfulness can turn a negative situation into a positive one. It can also open your heart to the beauty around you.

EXERCISES: BEING GRATEFUL

Review your entire life with the attitude of thankfulness. Feel gratitude for each event in your life, even if you're not sure exactly what you are thankful for. It's never too late to transform your past. A bad childhood is only a point of view; it's never too late to have a good childhood. Anything is good if it has value, and being thankful gives value to your life.

Visualize yourself in a beautiful place in nature. Envision people whom you presently know, as well as people you have known in the past and see them entering into that beautiful place one by one. Allow a feeling of appreciation for each individual to fill you, flowing from your heart to their heart. Imagine stating out loud to each individual why you are thankful for their being in your life. This exercise has the power to transform your life completely.

Give Thanks for Your Body

If you are in need of healing, being thankful for your body can help open the door to healing. When you pray for healing, sometimes it can come from the point of view that your body isn't okay. Subconsciously your body hears this and often responds in a negative way. If you radiate love and thankfulness for your body, it often responds by becoming healthier.

To better understand how this works, imagine a child whose parents are constantly wishing that she would stop being so bad. When the child hears these negative comments, she often fulfills her parents' expectations and responds by being "bad." However, if the parents are appreciative and thankful for their child, she will often respond in a positive manner. Go through your body, part by part, with a feeling of thankfulness. Thank your heart, your eyes, and your teeth. Thank your immune system. Thank each part of your body. The more parts of your body you thank, the stronger effect it will have on your body.

Give Thanks for Nature and the Creator

It has been said that when Native Americans first heard of setting aside only one day to worship God, they were concerned. They said, "The Great Mystery is everywhere. All our days are filled with worship of the beauty of God's creation." When a woman gathering herbs in the forest saw the great spread of an eagle's wings silhouetted against the sun, she would pause for a moment with the feeling of worship and thankfulness in her heart. When a hunter saw a great massive cedar tree spanning its branches into the sky, he would stop and feel a sense of gratefulness fill him. There was no need to set one day apart, since all days were holy.

Whatever you admire outside yourself will begin to grow within you. For example, if you feel a deep fulfilling gratitude for the old gnarled oak tree that has again and again survived the trials of time, you begin to imbue within yourself the qualities of strength and endurance. Whatever qualities you focus your attention on, in the spirit of gratefulness, will begin to grow within you. Whenever you are thankful to the Creator, the love and energy of the Creator will expand within you. This is a universal law. It's important to remember to give thanks for what you've gained by sharing it with others.

Step 5: Call for a Vision

Through the simplest alteration of consciousness you can enter into other realms on your Quest. When this occurs, the way you see the world around you begins to shift and change. Sometimes reality has an illusionary quality to it and time seems to stretch and contract. Things are not always as they seem. At the point when this occurs, you stand ready to embark upon a spiritual awakening, deepen your connection to Spirit, and gain clarity regarding your future direction. It's also during this time that you can heal emotional wounds and gain compassion and tranquillity. This final step is covered in the next chapter.

CHAPTER FIVE

CALLING FOR A VISION

It's time. You have created your sacred circle. You have prepared yourself mentally and emotionally. You are now ready to call for a vision.

This is an awesome and sacred moment. You stand at a threshold between two worlds. Before you lies a vast new horizon of beauty, mystery, and wonder. Behind you lies your past. In the moment that you let go of the cord that connects you to your former life, you step into a realm beyond linear time. Crossing through the mystic gateway may be dramatic and inspiring or it may occur softly like a whispered breeze. However, once you have crossed over you may not go back. Though the form of your outer life may stay the same, your inner life will never be the same.

A vision can take many forms, from a deep insight, to a dream, to a physical manifestation. There are two common ways to call for a vision. One is active and one is passive. Active calling for a vision is called beseeching. This means that you are actively pursuing and asking for a vision. The second way is to be passive and open and wait. There are advantages to each way.

Beseeching

Beseeching means to pray or speak from your heart to the Divine. The words you use are less important than the sincerity of your spirit. You can speak, chant, or sing your prayers. You can call out loudly and plaintively. You can silently invoke the Creator without words, directly from your heart. You don't need to be eloquent or explain yourself. Be real. Be honest. Be sincere. To beseech is to actively ask for help and guidance. The best way to call for a vision is to be very focused and yet relaxed at the same time. A chant I use is "Thy will and my will be one," so that what I receive will be in harmony with the Creator's plan for my life.

Black Elk, a Native American holy man born in the 19th century, was interviewed in 1947 about his Vision Quest. He talked about staking out a sacred circle for a Vision Quest and then walking back and forth and calling out the traditional cry for a vision, "O Great Spirit, be merciful to me, that my people may live."[1] This deeply felt cry to the heavens reminds the vision seekers that their vision is not just for themselves, but it's for the good of all beings. We're all related. It's important that you're not just beseeching for yourself but for "all relations." If you cry for a vision for the benefit of all, the heavens will cascade blessings upon you.

When imploring for a vision, you can call for guidance from the Spirit realm to help you. A simple way to do this is to say, "May the spirits, guides, ancestors, and angels that have gathered in peace bring love and guidance. I give thanks for the help that is given. May what is received be for the good of all."

Spirit guides. Personal guides are often those who have been with you in previous lifetimes and who feel kinship and unconditional love for you. They've been on the earth plane before, so they understand the difficulties and challenges of living on the earth and can offer valuable support. They're excellent to call on if you're struggling with earthly issues.

Ancestors. Native cultures honor ancestors and believe that they offer assistance, especially in times of need. It's not uncommon to have your ancestors watching over you on a Quest. They're very good to call, especially if you're dealing with family issues.

Angels. Angels can bring a message of hope and love, especially on your Quest. They radiate a celestial energy and give love and guidance. It's especially wonderful to ask for angelic energies while calling for a vision. I've heard remarkable stories of angelic encounters on Quests.

Allies. Allies can come in different forms. The most common ally is your totem animal. You can call on your spirit animal helper to assist you. For example, if you need to have an overview of your life, you might call upon the spirit of the eagle: "Brother Eagle, help me see my world with your clarity."

The advantage of beseeching lies in the action. If you're the kind of person who passively waits for opportunities to come your way, and they don't ever come, then taking action might be the best path for you. To manifest your dreams, often you need to take action. Go for it. Reach for the stars. If you're having a difficult time on your Quest, beseeching can help you through it. Just keep praying harder and harder until the difficulty eases. The disadvantage of beseeching for a vision might be that you miss a simple and direct message from Spirit because you are so focused on your requests.

Open and Accept

The second way to call for a vision is to still your mind, be open, and accept whatever occurs. Transformation and change don't often come in the way that we expect. In fact, it's often because it's *not* as we expected that we can be transformed. Be open. Expect the unexpected. Revel in the unfolding of each new day. Often it's in the quiet moments of life that remarkable insights occur. Accept. Receive. Breathe. Observe. Just be. The most common way that visions appear is through intuition, a spontaneous thought or just an inner knowing. Visions don't usually come as a lightning-bolt realization but rather as a gentle emerging awareness. To encourage your vision, be conscious of the thoughts that float through your mind. Very often, the simple exercise of watching your thoughts can provide remarkable insights into your life and your future.

The advantage of being quiet and open is that you can hear the whispers from spirit. If you're the kind of person who is constantly on the go and actively pursuing goals, just sitting and being can be an ideal way for you to experience a vision. The disadvantage of being still is that sometimes it creates boredom and restlessness. While you are trying to "be" in the moment, your mind is filling with mental chatter about seemingly unimportant things. When you just sit, you might feel tired and or distracted. If you have difficulty ignoring the distractions, just say to yourself, *And this too.* This simple statement allows you to acknowledge the mental diversion, so that you can let it go. What you resist persists, so instead of resisting distractions, simply acknowledge them to let them go. Distractions are a part of your Quest. They can also teach you about yourself. The way you deal with them allows you to gain spiritual power and depth.

How Visions Occur

A vision can occur in many different forms. It can occur quietly, even beyond your conscious recognition, or it can be dramatic and moving. No matter in what form the vision occurs for you, it expands the parameters of your life. It can come through the signs in the natural world around you, your dreams, or even in a manifested physical form. The form is less important than how the vision affects you. All visions change your life.

Watch the Signs

One of the ways the Creator answers prayers and grants visions is through signs. This is why it's so important to be still and to listen and observe everything. Often your vision can come directly from the changes and movements of nature in your Quest area. When watching for signs, observe the creatures, large and small, around your Quest site. Particularly notice anything that seems unusual. For example, if a bird that is normally timid comes near your site, or if you see an owl in the middle of the day (owls usually are active only at night), these occurrences may contain hidden meaning. Even ordinary occurrences can be part of your vision. A lone hawk making lazy circles in the sky, an ant tugging something much larger than itself along the dirt, a sudden rise in the wind—all these common events can contain deep meaning for your life.

Watch and listen to the plant life around you. Watch the millions of stars and other planets revolving around their suns, other worlds, and other life-forms. Even insects near your Quest site can carry special messages for you. Listening to the soft murmurs of the wind, often you can catch a whispered word or hear a personal message. The clouds, especially at sunset, can take on a formation that carries a sign to you. When you take time to really observe your environment, you can discover something that applies uniquely to your life.

If you're unsure what the sign means, ask yourself, *If I knew what this sign was telling me, what might it be?* Often this can help you decipher the sign. Sometimes the messages and visions that you receive through signs are immediately apparent, but others may take months or even years to unravel. It's often the sign that takes years to comprehend fully that is the most valuable. Your Vision Quest never ends. The visions and messages that you receive through signs go on throughout your life.

Visions appearing in clouds are a very common occurrence. After a recent Quest I led, six participants came to me to tell me about the great cloud angel they had seen. It was amazing to hear their stories. From different parts of the island, and unknown to one another, they had all seen the same cloud formation, which looked like large magnificent angel. Though each individual had a different perspective, all were in awe of the grand beauty of this remarkable phenomenon.

Erika Klement, a therapist from Australia, wrote me about a remarkable vision that appeared to her in the clouds:

> *By the end of the first day I felt a little hungry but it soon passed. I looked toward the sunset, and the clouds seemed to be shaped like people running to it. It was like being drawn in; back into the beginning of time. The message I heard was,*

"We're all going back into Oneness now, no matter what we do or what we feel, we're all going home." What a wonderful end to the day on which I had asked to receive a vision.

Greg, a sales executive from Texas, watched the pink clouds of sunset shifting and changing form as the sun lowered on the horizon. One cloud formation looked like a phoenix with great vast wings that seemed to dive into another cloud formation that looked like a huge fire. As he watched the "fire" cloud it seemed to dissolve into an opening flower. Greg felt that it was a powerful message for him. He felt that the phoenix symbolized that he was in the process of transforming into another kind of human being, and that his heart was opening like the flower opening to the sun.

Keith Wicks, a British certified accountant for a Japanese shipping company, told me the following story about his request for signs from the Creator. This experience happened immediately after his Quest, during the integration period:

I asked, "Please show me a sign to prove I am on the right path." After about 30 seconds a bat flew into my tepee. Initially shocked, I watched it circle inside, not hitting anything. Several minutes later it eventually found its exit. . . . Realizing I had asked for a sign, I went to the library in the lodge to look up the symbolism of the bat. Finding the chapter on the bat, it started with the word <u>Rebirth.</u> . . . Rebirth was exactly right for me. Most of my friends are now bored silly with me recounting this story, but there were so many more lessons I learned on those ten days of the Vision Quest seminar. Actually, I am still learning from them. The implications to me have yet to find limits.

Renate Nordby, from Norway, watched a slug and a woodpecker, which were purveyors of signs that gave her profound insight about her life:

A long slug, unprotected, innocent and soft, made its way across the center of my circle. I watched that little creature moving, taking its own time to reach its destination. It moved slowly but determinedly. It made its way straight ahead without any rest or hesitation. At the same time in a neighboring tree just outside my circle a woodpecker was pecking at a tremendous speed on the bark of the tree. [I noticed that both animals were moving at their own speed and said to myself,] "From today I will act and move in my own speed. By moving at my own speed I can keep in touch with both my intuition and my creativity, which gives me the strength to keep in focus and be centered and determined. . . . I shall love rushing people and respect them for having their own speed. However, I shall love and respect myself for my speed and personal rhythm."

When watching the signs to gain a vision, observe the symbols that appear to you. Susan L. Schrotenboer, a consultant from Arizona, found that her sign was a symbol formed by the trees near her Vision Quest spot. This had a deep and lasting meaning for her:

Two trees grew low on the cliff so that their branches were at eye level when I sat in the center of my medicine circle. On my right was an evergreen tree that I felt symbolized the eternity of life. On my left was a deciduous tree, symbolizing the cycles of life. The branches met in such a way as to form a frame for my view. On the second day of my Vision Quest, I sat looking across the channel, watching raindrops dancing on the water and birds swooping for fish. I realized that the frame of branches I was looking through formed a heart. This made me groan because I have always thought that this common symbol for love was trite. Why did this shape appear in my life at that time? From the center of my circle I looked through a heart and watched the world. I realized that the message was, "I must turn off the mind chatter and open my heart. I must look at the world with a view from the heart."

One week after returning from my Vision Quest, I was strolling through an arts and crafts fair. I found a handcrafted, sterling silver heart-shaped pin that wasn't completely closed at the point. I now wear it as a reminder to keep my heart open. I make sure I wear it when I know I am going to be in a confrontational or negative situation. Learning to live through my heart has changed my thought patterns dramatically and created miracles in how I relate to other people. It has been particularly helpful during job interviews and traveling to new places.

Your vision can come as a direct communication from the signs. In every moment, Spirit's whispering to you through signs. Judge nothing. Be open to everything. Watch. Listen. Feel. Signs will unfold around you.

Listen to Your Dreams

Your vision can come in your dreams so it's very important to take note of all the dreams you have while on your Quest. If you're not in a habit of remembering your dreams, before you go to sleep repeat over and over to yourself: "Tonight I remember my dreams." Often this is enough to begin to be aware of your nocturnal journeys. Another dream-recall technique is to doodle in your journal immediately on awakening. This can activate the creative, nonlinear part of your brain and stimulate recall.

Sometimes dream visions come in a symbolic form that needs to be deciphered; however, some dream visions are easily understood and very clear. Herman, a mechanical engineer from Germany, said that his dream vision was extraordinarily clear. In his dream his grandmother, who had raised him, was holding him and rocking him while she sat in a large rocking chair outdoors on a clear night. He remembered watching the stars when suddenly all of them started to move and formed into these words: *open doors*. He woke from his dream knowing that his mission in life was to "open doors" for other people. He had practiced yoga for a number of years and was considering teaching yoga. He felt that his dream was a sign to teach yoga to help open doors for others.

One woman, from Africa, had dreams during her Quest that had a profound effect on her. She dreamed several times of being an eagle and woke up wondering:

What did my dreams signify? Why didn't I seem able to get the message? Groping for some water, I sipped some and looked out across the ocean to the reddening horizon. All of a sudden I stared transfixed. There, unmistakably, was a massive eagle wing of crimson cloud stretched above the dark sleeping island in the distance. Each feather was etched in brilliant crimson and gold as the sky brightened. It was so vivid and real but my dizzy head could not begin to grapple with its significance. What was this? I asked Great Spirit and my constant spirit companion to help me understand these signs. Immediately I saw, with crystal clarity, the head of a proud Native American, his bronzed features, the feathers about his head and his red clothing about his shoulders, clear and vivid. Who are you? You have a message I can't decipher! With that, the sun burst over the horizon and melted the image.

I sat up feeling very unsteady and reached for my notebook, frantically wanting to take down his message. One of the most important reasons I had come on the Quest had not yet been satisfied. I still didn't know the names of any of my guides, whose daily presence around me I had grown so accustomed to. I questioned and wrote, scribbling in a daze as the answers came. "What is your name?" (I heard the name Aywa.) "And what is my name?" (I heard the name Eagle Feather.) How blind could I be! How much clearer could any message be? Had I once been a Native American then? The deep peace I was feeling was certainly like coming home. "What have you to tell me?" I asked. I heard the answer, "You have the powerful gifts of healing and compassion. Your ultimate destination is one with all. Accept yourself in your perfect beauty." My soul was alive with a depth of emotion I had never before experienced, my heart bursting with a warmth that filled my whole being, and my circle seemed aglow with a brilliant radiance.

Manifestations

Sometimes a vision manifests in a powerful physical way. In a heightened or altered state of consciousness archetypal images can appear. A large boulder becomes a crouched giant, a tree becomes a sage, a cloud becomes an angel, a twig becomes a serpent. A spirit name is heard. A power song is received. Totem animals materialize. A voice speaks out of the darkness. The unexplained and mysterious occur. Although these aren't normal experiences, the fact that they do happen gives credence to the idea that there are spiritual forces propelling us along our path. Deborah, a therapist from London, had quite a remarkable manifestation experience on her Quest.

During the Vision Quest it became very apparent that my seven-year relationship would have to change, possibly end. The clarity of this realization was absolute. It felt as if a huge burden had lifted from my shoulders. Until that moment I had not consciously realized how destructive the relationship had become, for both of us. I remember sitting in my circle feeling lighter and more alive than I had ever experienced. It felt like I was at peace with everyone and everything, no separation, no body. I have no idea how long this lasted. It could have been a second or a lifetime. Everything was possible in that moment. I wasn't thinking; just being. It remains beyond the powers of my description.

The next thing I remember is laughing out loud with such a sense of liberation. My mind switched back in and was desperately trying to make sense of it all. It was full of questions and doubts. I thought, What if this is a kind of madness? I focused myself and became aware of the rise and fall of my breath, letting my mind gradually become a little stiller. I tried to watch my thoughts and not get involved with them. I became aware of my surroundings, the sounds and smells, the feel of the moss beneath me. Some birds were calling to each other from the pine trees on either side of me. I focused on their song, it was so beautiful. Just then I saw something flutter right in front of me.

A bird flew no more than 18 inches away from me at eye level. I followed where it went and as it flew towards a nearby tree, another bird joined it.

I wondered if these were the birds I had been listening to, but I didn't have time to think, as they seemed to be putting on a display for me—at least that's how it felt. They flew between two trees, sometimes together, sometimes alone, dipping and calling. It was so natural and simple, but so beautiful, and I was full of a sense of wonder and honor for the majesty of nature. The birds were now both lodged in a tree about four feet away from me. They had been silent and still for a few minutes. I thought that the display had come to an end but my body felt electric and expectant. What happened next is still so vivid, and yet impossible in some ways to describe.

Just as I thought it was over, the birds emerged from the tree, swooping down together, as if synchronized, matching wing beat for wing beat. They were only a couple of inches apart; this in itself looked spectacular. Then I realized they were coming in my direction. It all happened so fast. As they got closer, they pulled apart, still keeping their unity of movement. I stared in disbelief at what happened then, for as they separated, in the space between them grew the most beautiful beaded net! Each end of which was held in either beak. This net was the most beautiful thing I have ever seen. It had a luminosity that shimmered in the light, and at each intersection was a beautiful blue bead, a color between turquoise and lapis. I just stared open-mouthed. The birds circled around me and then flew directly overhead, and as they did, they dropped the net over me. I felt its impact as it landed. Blinking, I looked and felt around for the net, but it was nowhere to be seen. It had only taken an instant. I couldn't possibly have fallen asleep. It certainly didn't feel like a dream.

I sat there, unable to take in or explain what I had experienced. I felt washed new. I had been shown the strength and protection that was available to me. I knew that I would have the capability to follow through with the changes that I needed to make in my life. I gave thanks to Spirit for giving me such a beautiful experience. As a result of my Quest I feel a stronger sense of connection to all those around me and a greater sense of responsibility for all my actions. The challenges of life are as present as ever, however; I just get out of the hole a little quicker each time.

Linton Pope, a television producer from South Africa, had a very powerful experience in which he faced something that was so foreign to his rational mind that it shifted his perception of reality forever.

I have never encountered a process as powerful as a Vision Quest. Through the years I have studied many philosophies and teachings, and have been through many forms of experiential processes. None has come close to the effect of a Vision Quest.

Upon arriving on the island I was faced with a hurdle—the group of people who had come to do the Quest were not my idea of "Vision Questers." During the days [on the island] prior to the actual Quest, buried emotional issues began to surface. I felt out of control! My intellectual process was disintegrating.

The evening arrived to depart on my Quest. It was a very scary yet thrilling feeling. I wanted desperately to begin my solitude but simultaneously wanted to find the nearest canoe and paddle to [the nearest town]. My first night out there was an ego kick. I was Mr. Tough, Mr. Pioneer. The first day dawned and I felt extreme elation. The first day soon became a little boring and irritating. I found my mind was jumping all over the place. I seriously began to question why I was there.

The second night came and went, mixed with shadows of fear and insecurity. The second day saw everything becoming more intense, to the point that I was extremely angry and holding back a well of tears. I felt as though I was dying in a sense.

The night soon fell and my emotions seemed to intensify even further. Somewhere in the middle of the night I decided that nothing would stop me and I left my circle. The forest suddenly became dark and intimidating. I cautiously made my way through the woods toward the other side of the island. All of a sudden I heard what sounded like an entire herd of elephants charging through the forest, and they were coming directly at me! I stood transfixed! This was not possible, as the island was small and had only deer and smaller creatures as its inhabitants. The sound grew louder and louder until it was deafening. I ran to a tree and stood with my back to it, hopefully preventing myself from being crushed in the stampede that was now seconds away from flattening me.

I had grown up in the African bush and knew the sounds and dangers of such an event. Suddenly, in a flash, the entire forest became so silent that you could almost hear the stars twinkling. Then a deep male voice boomed my surname, "Pope." It was said in a very stern and reprimanding way. My legs almost collapsed. I remember thinking, "Now you have really flipped out, Linton." However, I was lucid and anything but delirious. Terrified, yes, but fully awake and aware. After the voice boomed my name the forest fell silent again as though nothing had happened.

I stood paralyzed for what felt like an eternity. Who had shouted my name, who was watching me, what in God's name created a stampede out of nothing and then made it vaporize instantly? Did Denise have sound equipment hidden in the trees with scouts watching each person's movement? As paranoid as these thoughts were, they were easier to digest than any other possibilities.

Finally, I made my way back to my circle and entered with a new sense of respect that I was at a loss to explain. Not only was my intellect useless but my mind was now skating on razor blades. Somehow I knew that what I had just experienced was not the result of a clever illusion on the part of any human being. This absolute knowing seemed to shift the perspective of my entire universe.

The dawn approached and I remember praying that this would all end. I wanted out of this place. I hated it with a deep passion. The day was the longest of my life. I drifted in and out of strange states and thoughts. I felt this desperate sense of aloneness that nothing could ever fix. I was truly lost and desperate. In simplistic terminology I wanted my mommy! Images of my mother began to surface, most of which were uncomfortable and irritating. I desperately needed to touch another human being. I spent the rest of the day anticipating my return to the camp. My anger seemed to have shifted into a mixed feeling of love and tolerance.

Sunset and the time to return arrived at last. I gathered my sleeping bag and suddenly I was overcome by a huge sense of loss as I left the circle. I felt as though I was leaving home. I seemed barely able to walk. I felt as though I was gliding across the hill and the further I got from the circle the more the tears began to fall. It felt as though everything seemed to be pouring out from inside me. My body became lighter and lighter. I wanted the walk back to camp to take as long as possible. I was overcome by an intense feeling of freedom, joy, and sadness, a state of bliss.

Finally I arrived at the camp to find Janna [another Quest participant]. We sat in silence for a long time, watching the other people drift in from all over. I looked at each one in astonishment. They all had the most beautiful expressions on their faces and seemed to be surrounded by an exceptionally harmonious energy of some kind. Gradually we all hugged each other, and for the first time in my life I looked forward to a hug from another human being. As I hugged each person I could feel their harmony and most importantly my own harmony, accompanied by a tremendous sense of peace.

The desire on everyone's part to hug and be hugged was deafening. The most amazing observation was that no one said a word. There was absolutely no need to. What was needed was simply being done, instead of it being spoken about. It was, by far, the most electrifying silence I have ever experienced. It was a very sad good-bye the day we all left; these people were no longer the strangers whom I judged, but intimate souls that had risked their very being, in the name of truth. This creates a bond that lasts forever!

If You Didn't Receive a Vision

One returning Quest participant said, "Nothing happened on my Vision Quest." I asked, "Do you mean that you weren't caressed by morning mists, and the night sky wasn't filled with a vast landscape of stars? You didn't hear the lapping of gentle waves against the shore, and the frogs didn't sing at night?" She laughed and said, "I mean, I didn't have a real vision." I replied, "If you went on a Vision Quest with an open heart, you had a real vision. Accept your vision in whatever form it came to you, even if it isn't what you expected. Acknowledge it. Honor it and give thanks for what was given."

Our expectations are a result of childhood programming and preconditioned responses. On your Quest you are embracing a new way of being in the world, where expectations and old patterns of the past drop away. Growth, transformation, and change do not always fit expectations!

Rich in symbolism, steeped in beauty, everything that you experience on your Quest is a magical part of your vision. In ways that perhaps are beyond the awareness of your five senses, seeds are planted in the fertile soil of soul that will bear fruit in the years to come, even if you have uncertainty about the form that your vision took. On your Quest you appealed to the Creator, to your spirit allies, and to your higher self. Trust that the way in which they answered your prayers was the best way for you. The way to receive a vision is to accept and surrender to whatever happens on your Vision Quest. Jaap de Kreek, from Holland, said this about his Quest.

> There I was, sitting on the cold earth, watching the pouring rain covering an empty bay. I prayed for a spark of sun and thought about the many pleasures of my luxurious life back home.
>
> I waited for the big moment of enlightenment. Nothing happened. Nothing at all, not even the slightest miracle.
>
> Two days were filled with absolutely nothing but silence. Since I had one day left, I decided to quit trying to call for a

vision. Instead I decided to spend my remaining time simply enjoying myself. At the time it really didn't feel like a choice . . . it just happened.

There and then my life changed!

In that moment, in my circle of stones, my lifelong belief system of needing to struggle and make an effort to achieve success changed. I felt a deep sense of peace fill me. Those days in the beauty of silence brought me to the decision to leave my successful work and to sell my flourishing company. I challenged myself to break through the comforting shields of my daily life, and use my time for growth and adventure.

For me, my Vision Quest was not only a distillation of my 54 years of existence but also a turning point in life. In the year since the Quest I have sold my business and I feel free. I can't hide behind my work and my growing success in the world anymore. I have much more time to go deeper into myself, and now life seems to be an ongoing adventure.

Completing Your Quest

Send Prayers for Others and the Planet

No matter what form your Quest took, on a deep level you amassed spiritual energy. It's extremely valuable to project this energy to others. Complete your Quest by sending prayers, blessings, and good thoughts toward people you know and love. Then send prayers to people that you don't know and perhaps will never know. Then send prayers to all creatures of our beautiful planet and to the planet, Mother Earth, herself.

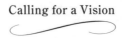
Clean Up

Before you start to take apart your circle, it's important to give thanks to the spirits of that place and to the unseen helpers who gave you guidance. Take time to put the area back in its natural state. Make it look as completely natural as possible. If there's rubbish that is not yours in the surrounding area, take it with you when you leave as a gracious way of giving thanks to the spirit of the place where you had your Quest.

The First Hours Back

It's very important to be gentle with yourself for the first hours and days after a Quest. This is a special time when you are making the transition back into everyday life, a time for reflection, integration, grounding, and rest. Some people feel ecstatic and exhilarated after a Quest. Such a response can mean that the individual isn't quite ready to return to regular life and they need some time to ground themselves. Some people feel exhausted, and for them it's important to rest. Don't complete your Quest and immediately jump back into life. Shorten your Quest rather than shorten the integration time after it, as the integration period is as important as the Quest. Take time to reflect, access, and remember what you have experienced.

Sharing with Others

Your Quest is not just for yourself. When you return, you're carrying sacred energy back for the good of all people. In Native American tradition, immediately after a Quest, the initiated individual sat among the elders in council, who heard the experience, discussed the meaning of it, and accepted that individual back into the tribe with new status. Often a name was conferred at that time, if one wasn't received on the Quest.

In the hours immediately after your Quest, be careful with whom you share your experience. Sometimes other people's views can distort your experience but other times people can add insight. If you decide to share your experiences, make sure the people you tell are supportive and willing to just listen without adding their interpretation. At times it can be better to keep the insights to yourself. Yet, at other times, sharing increases the value you gain. Trust your intuition on what is appropriate for you.

CHAPTER SIX

Vision Quests for Teenagers

In ancient times, Native American children, near the time of puberty, were sent on a Vision Quest as a ceremonial passage into adulthood. Primarily this rite was for boys between the ages of 10 and 17, but in some tribes girls were allowed to go as well. A Native American Vision Quest was an opportunity for adolescents to seek their spirit guides, find their inner strength, and discover life direction. Often, spiritual guidance would come to them in a dream or a vision, usually in the form of an animal. A typical Quest lasted four days and nights, and vision seekers underwent physical hardships, such as fasting, so the spirits would take pity on them. When the teen returned to the village with his vision, he was considered an adult. His newfound spirit guide would assist him throughout his life, helping him find his path.

Our modern society is lacking in rites of passage for teenagers, as they journey through different stages of development. The few ceremonies that we have in our society, such as graduation, don't usually touch the deep spiritual importance that accompanies significant transitions in life. However, the Vision Quest offers a powerful way for teenagers to honor their passage into adulthood and to gain clarity to their purpose and destiny. Meadow, my daughter, has been participating in Vision Quests since she was 13 years old. She wrote the remainder of this chapter when she was 17 years old, sharing her Quest experiences as well as comments of her friends who have been on Quests. This chapter is especially pertinent because it's a teenager writing to teenagers. Since the time that she originally wrote this chapter, Meadow (as an adult) has gone on to lead Quests for adolescents. In addition, she gives practical suggestions for any teenager who wishes to embark on this sacred path.

∾

Over the past five years, I've been on six quests in the United States in places such as Utah, Washington State, and New Hampshire. These Quests ranged in length from one to four days, and my first was in the Cascade Mountains of Washington State. I went with my mother and a group consisting mostly of adults, though there were three other teenagers. I was tremendously excited but also a little nervous. Looking back, I realize that I did not fully understand the exact meaning of a Quest. When the day finally came, we woke up before dawn and drove in silence to a high vantage point to spend the next 24 hours in solitude. We unloaded the vans just as the sun was rising over the horizon, collected our necessary gear, and walked off in different directions in search of our sites. The morning air still cool, our breath left white clouds in the air. While I looked for my "perfect" site, a voice in my head kept telling me to look for apparitions, ghosts, and the paranormal. To me, a vision had meant a hallucination or a booming voice from above giving me wisdom and telling me my purpose.

I finally found a site on the top of a grassy hill, facing Mt. Rainier, the highest point in Washington State. I set up camp, made my circle, and sprinkled cornmeal around the periphery to help create a sacred space as my mother had told me to do. In case I couldn't endure the 24 hours without food, I sereptiously saved some of the cornmeal. Once I had finished with all the necessary preparations, I sat in the grass and stared at the mountain in the distance, waiting for my vision to come. I waited and waited. It was very hot, so I drank some water, and then I waited some more. The sun was pounding on my bare shoulders, so I put on sunblock and then waited some more.

I had read in history books about saints having visions, so I expected a miracle or something special to happen to me, too. I didn't understand that a vision didn't have to be anything grandiose. A vision could be a realization about myself or overcoming my fears. I tried so hard to have an "amazing experience" that I wasn't sensitive to what I was gaining from spending time alone.

I kept hoping to see something out of the ordinary, like a deer walking over to me and lying in my circle or clouds moving just because I willed them to do so. But the only thing that disturbed the silence was the growling of my stomach. Exasperated, my thoughts were going crazy.

"I'm still here. Where's my Vision?"

"I'm hungry. Where are you, Vision?"

"I'm really bored . . . and hungry. I'm not going to wait around for you, Vision!"

The hunger grew to the point that it was the only thing on my mind. I remembered the bag of cornmeal I had set aside for an emergency. I retrieved it from my backpack and doused it with water in a vain attempt to make something edible. I set the wet mush on a rock in the sun, trying to make corn chips. I couldn't wait for the mush to dry; I just *had* to eat it. I'll never forget how it tasted. It had the texture of sandpaper and the taste of moist dust, getting stuck in my teeth and in the back of my throat.

Although I kept hoping a vision would still appear, I became so preoccupied with food that I finally left my circle and snuck into the base camp and took a couple pieces of barbecued chicken that had been left out. I can't remember any food ever tasting as good. I felt a bit guilty about eating it. However, later my mom said she was still proud of me because I had overcome my natural timidity when I took the chicken. She said that was valuable in itself.

Even though I didn't have the type of vision I expected, nevertheless I gained a great deal from my first Vision Quest experience. When I packed up my site, I felt like I left the young timid Meadow behind and emerged more confident and sure of myself. I was proud of myself for surviving 24 hours alone. That was something I had never done before. The other three teenagers in the group were the only adolescents I knew at the time who had ever spent so much time in solitude. It made me feel proud that we had done something that most teenagers never attempt. Since that time I have realized that it's not necessary to have an incredible experience or a vision like the type I had imagined. This realization has made my other Quests more powerful.

Later I did Quests with organizations that specialized in teenage trips. They refer to a Quest as a *solo* because this word emphasizes being solo in nature, as opposed to searching for enlightenment, or a "vision." I think that it would have helped me when I was 13 to have called my time alone in nature a solo rather than a Vision Quest. While a deeper understanding of self is certainly obtained from a solo, for most teenagers the name *solo* is less intimidating than Vision Quest. I prefer using the word *solo* for teenage Quests because it diminishes the stress of having to find a vision.

My longest solo, four days, was part of a semester program at the Mountain School in Vermont, a boarding school I attended in my junior year. (The Mountain School is a high school with regular academic classes but also teaches about nature, organic farming, and animal husbandry.) During my time there our teachers prepared us for our solos by teaching us how to bandage wounds in case something unforeseen happened, how to build a shelter in the event of bad weather, and how to deal with the inevitable boredom of being alone in the woods for four days. After much preparation, 45 students were taken into the forest and placed along various woodland streams to spend four days and three nights.

I spent the four days sitting and thinking. I mostly thought about things that seemed mundane at the time, especially considering my surroundings. Most of the time I felt relaxed and content but I was also worried that my 44 friends, also alone in the woods, were gaining the "secrets of the universe" while I was just sitting.

However, when it was over, I emerged from the woods feeling a great sense of accomplishment. I had never spent that much time in complete silence and solitude. It was one of the most moving experiences I've ever had. In many respects it gave me a perspective about who I am and my direction for the rest of my life. The confidence I gained by knowing I had the courage to be alone in the woods carried over into my entire life. I'd generally been shy around peers and rarely showed outward affection. On my solo I realized how important my friends are to me. I began to initiate hugs, and invite people over to my home. I no longer worried that people didn't want to spend time with me. My classmates at the Mountain School had similar experiences. Some gained insight about their life and others learned an appreciation for the land. I have asked my friends to share their experiences with me. The quotes in this chapter are excerpted from the journals they took on their solos.

The Importance of Solos for Teenagers

The main events that will mark my growing up will have been getting my driver's license at 16 and graduating from high school at 18. The next monumental occasion in my life to mark my maturity will be turning 21 and being permitted to drink legally. These aren't necessarily satisfying or empowering rites of passage. We don't currently have a traditional teenage ceremonial honoring of transition that distinguishes childhood from adulthood, in this country, in the same way that a Quest does. I believe my true rites of passage have been the Quests and solos I have done. I feel more mature after each one because new levels of self-knowledge emerge. These are some of reasons why it's valuable for modern teenagers to spend time alone in nature on a solo:

- Learning to be alone with yourself
- Evaluating your role in society
- Feeling a sense of independence
- Gaining inner peace
- Overcoming your fears
- Learning the value of solitude
- Truly experiencing nature
- Having time away from the clock and commitments
- Getting to know yourself better

Learning to Be Alone with Yourself

Most teenagers are not accustomed to being alone. I'm an only child, but still I'm rarely alone. I'm at school between 7 to 14 hours a day, then I go home to my parents. When I'm at home alone, I often fill the silence with the radio, a novel, the television, or telephone conversations. I seldom just sit and think, letting my mind wander.

I think it's important for me (and for teenagers in general) to realize that it's okay to be alone. It's all right to "space out," stare at a blade of grass, daydream, or whatever else you feel like doing. Abigail Chatfield, a student from the Mountain School, puts it succinctly: "It's such a strange feeling; not thinking, [just] sitting and spacing out; it's so unproductive." While some people may feel that just sitting is unproductive, my Native American ancestors sat in stillness in nature "not thinking" in order to gain insight and knowledge. It was the art of being alone that allowed for those ancient Quests to be powerful turning points in life and eased the individual's integration into adult tribal life.

Evaluating Your Role in Society

Our high school years are a time for us to define who we are and to determine our role in society. A solo is a good time for teens to separate themselves from their community and look at it from the outside with a different perspective. On her Mountain School solo, Allison Cohen questioned how modern teenagers have chosen to live their lives:

> I wonder what would happen if I tried to live my life the way I'm living now. Could I do it? Would I ever want to do it? I'm doing exactly what I want to do moment by moment. I have my lemonade, my book, and my journal in my bag. Sometimes I sit and "be," sometimes I read, sometimes I sing, sometimes I write in my journal, sometimes I get up and dance around a

little and then sometimes I eat or drink. The only thing that governs which of those things I do is what I feel like doing. I'm realizing how little time I spend really doing what I want to do. Most of the time I do what I should be doing and I make myself believe that it's what I want to do. Maybe they're the same thing. I really wonder if I could just live each moment as it comes, as I am now. Would I be happy doing that? Could I survive? Is that really how we're supposed to be living and we've just messed everything up?

As a result of this solo, Allison has spent time determining her priorities in her future life, and this has given her a deeper sense of the role that she will play in society.

Feeling a Sense of Independence

For some teenagers the feeling of independence and accomplishment of being able to survive alone in the wilderness is as powerful as the actual experience of solo. Sarah writes, "I was permitted to go to the Mountain School with the repeated condition that I could not go on solo. I had the biggest fight I have ever had with my parents about this. I resented their involvement. Solo was something I really wanted to experience, and they refused. I was finally permitted to go on solo provided our leaders, Pat and Holly, could see me from the base camp." Sarah wrote in her journal at the end of her solo, "Looking back I realize what going on solo meant to me. It meant complete independence."

For Sarah, solo represented being trusted to make her own decisions and assess a situation on her own. Solo is often the first time a teenager has spent away from home on their own, away from the dictates of others. On solo you do exactly what you feel compelled to do in the moment, and that can feel liberating.

Gaining Inner Peace

Ben Pomeroy felt that the solitude in nature on solo allowed him a deeper sense of peace. In his journal he wrote:

> *For the past few days I have been living a simple and enjoyable life. Waking up with the sun, making strong tea and eating cheese and bread for breakfast. My day is dictated by my hunger, sleeping desires, and inclinations. Nothing much has worried me, except an occasional rain cloud. I have reached a level of calmness and peace. Quite simple activities, like reading or drawing by the stream, are most enjoyable to me right now. Gone are the bright lights and loud noises, sharp edges, and foul smells. Here is a world of perfection and simplicity, where one may just sit and observe the soft beauty of his surroundings to achieve happiness.*
>
> *I feel like I am a Buddhist monk on a mission of revelation or a young Indian boy on a Vision Quest. I'm alone in nature with my basic necessities, nothing more. I have left the distractions and temptations of civilization to return to where I might find peace, harmony, and a balance between myself and nature. It's possible to co-exist harmoniously with the natural world, if one is wise and respectful.*

When doing a solo, teenagers usually focus on keeping warm, remaining hydrated, feeding their stomachs (if they choose to eat), and releasing the wealth of thoughts that they've been storing in their minds.

Usually the anxiety about school or the English paper they should write, the calculus assignment that is due, or the impending college applications, all drift away. The things that usually fill their minds at home seem very far away. They realize that most of the things that they're usually concerned about aren't really very important. Of course, when they get off their solo, they'll probably have to write the paper, do the math, and fill out the applications, but those tasks seem easier after a solo. There are very few things that we absolutely have to do in life . . . eat, drink, and stay

Overcoming Your Fears

The thought of spending hours alone in the woods can elicit a number of fears, many of which are conquered by the self-confidence gained with completion of the solo. Going out alone into the woods is an excellent way to face these fears and overcome them. For most teenagers the biggest fear is being alone. I believe that this is because as children our definition of self always comes from other people. Solo offers an opportunity to find out who you are without the definition from others.

Jessica Taverna explained her fear when she realized that she was completely alone:

I was putting any words I could think of onto the pages, anything to stave away <u>nothing.</u> As I wrote, my heart pounded, blood pulsed through my veins, and my hands shook, making it hard to grasp the pen. Fear was creeping into every bone and muscle in my body, into every inch of my soul as the words became scarce, the thoughts refusing to flow. This fear was strange, deeper than any I had ever felt. It went beyond worries about my tarp and my food.

It was fear of being alone with myself. Solitary, just me, nothing that had to be done, nothing to distract my mind from me. All the time in the world to think about myself. Within a couple of hours from the start of my solo, I knew the basic premise of what the next few days would hold. With only nature, myself, and a journal filled with stark white pages begging to be covered in words, I would be forced to confront the only person I had ever shied away from—<u>me.</u> This extended period of solitude offered me the opportunity to contemplate my interior self, what controlled my instinctual reactions to things, the virgin me, pure, unadulterated by the dictates of society. This was the part of myself that I hid, both from others, and often from *myself, the part of sadness and jealousy and hidden passions and insecurity and desire.*

Though Jessica went into her solo afraid of being alone and fearful of what she would find within herself, she finished it with a deep feeling of accomplishment. She pushed through the fear and found her hidden self. If she hadn't had the fear, she may have never realized that there was a part of her that she had hidden from herself and from others.

Teenagers who live in cities, like my friend Allison from New York City, who often have not spent much time in the wilderness, are usually particularly afraid of being alone. For these city teenagers, being alone at night in the woods can be quite frightening. Allison told me before she went out on her solo that she was even more afraid of being alone in the woods than she was of being out alone at night in New York City. She said that in New York you're most fearful when you're alone because then you're more likely to be mugged or approached by a stranger. She is safest on the streets when there are many people around. During her solo she felt that she overcame her fear of being alone and now she feels very comfortable in the woods and being by herself, though she is still cautious in New York City.

Gwyn Welles, a Mountain School student also from Manhattan, is like most teenagers. She's rarely alone. She constantly surrounds herself with others. She went off into the woods for her four-day solo wondering what she would do without a companion. Of this experience she says:

> *I was uncertain about how I was going to spend four days alone. I was nervous about 72 hours of no conversation except for the little voices that consult in my head. I did not question my survival; I had plenty of clothing and enough food to open a roadside stand. I did not fear being eaten by a bear. Survival of body I was certain of, tranquillity of mind I was not. I had never spent more than a day alone. Even then, it had been in the comfort of my own home. I realized, as we approached my solo site, that solitude was a companion I did not know very well.*

There's enormous power in a teenager realizing that she can overcome fear. Even overcoming one small fear on a solo can be a valuable step in learning how to overcome other fears that will occur later in life.

Learning the Value of Solitude

As Gwen overcame the initial fear of being alone, she realized that she could actually enjoy the solitude:

I have been with myself my entire life. So why was solitude a foreign state to me? I realized, as I took off my backpack and sat down . . . I rarely had been with myself. I did not know solitude because I had always avoided it. At age 6, I was first to arrive at the birthday parties, eager to play musical chairs. At 16, I forever was ready to gather a group for a game of Pictionary. On reflection, it's clear that I went to great lengths to guarantee that I was not alone. Being alone was awkward. If one is alone it's not out of choice, it's a result of rejection and denial. I remember when I was younger, sitting alone in my room and thinking to myself, What is wrong with me? I was unable to be happy when I was alone because I believed that I should have been somewhere else. To be alone was not important. To be alone was not natural.

At 17, I was finally encouraged to [go on solo and] be with myself. At this moment, to be alone was natural; to be alone was normal; to be alone was the only thing I could do. Perhaps I questioned solo less than other solitary experiences because I knew that 44 other people were alone in the woods drinking iodized stream water and sleeping under the stars, but for the first time, I allowed myself to look beyond the prologue of my situation, solitude, and I was able to discover the plot. I decided not to take many things out of my backpack. My novels remained resting under my sketchbook. Instead, I took thoughts out of boxes whose locks never knew that keys existed. Alone, without distraction, I was able to think about nothing but myself.

I discovered that to be alone is not to be lonely; it's not selfish, but truly liberating.

Truly Experiencing Nature

Many of us get caught up in our busy lives and forget to take time to appreciate the earth, the land that sustains us. Nature is an integral part of our lives; the trees create the air we breathe, the rivers and lakes supply us with water, the plants nourish us and the animals we eat. Even those of us who spend quite a bit of time in nature hiking and camping, often do not truly see nature. When I'm hiking, instead of experiencing the beauty of nature, I find that I spend the majority of my time staring at the ground to keep from tripping. The subtle sounds of the wilderness are masked by my talking to my hiking companions.

One of the only times that I can truly appreciate the natural world is when I'm on solo. Solo gives me the opportunity to study moss growing on a rock and the patterns leaves make after they have fallen to the ground. Ben examined his solo site quite closely and wrote about his discoveries in his journal:

> *The day is winding down and sun has begun its descent behind the mountains. A soft warm tone of yellow splashes through the forest. The kind of light only found in the late after-noon, when day is coming to a close, but allows us a few more hours of play before sunset. Maybe the clouds will be consider-ate and let me see sunset. These past few days have been a guessing game with sunshine or rain. Groton Forest seems to be a place that Mother Nature intended to be wild. These woods were once farmland. Old stone walls reveal boundaries of the past. They are now covered up by moss and overgrowth. Nature seems to mock the idea of property rights. Old apple trees in a meadow tell us of what is grown. The apple trees are now wild again, rejoining their counterparts as another piece of this mosaic arboretum. The meadow is overgrown and wild. Grass*

and weeds and wildflowers mingle together without fear of the farmer's tractor. What drove away these farmers? Did the poor soil of these hills save the woods?

When Sarah was finally allowed to do solo, she questioned how our society has veered away from all that is natural:

> *Even in this attempt to be in nature and of nature, I am constantly reminded how far removed I am. Looking at myself right now, sitting in a plastic shelter with a plastic ground sheet in my Crazy Creek chair and synthetic sleeping bag, cold, in my layers of polypro, wool, and fleece, is this really the closest I can get to nature? What does that say about my culture? We perceive ourselves as above nature, superior and controlling. Yet I can't survive alone in nature without carrying my pack filled with food and warmth. I can't even drink the water without putting chemicals in it.*

I believe that it's important for teenagers to be able to have the opportunity to spend time alone in nature. Perhaps if all young people did so and listened to the heartbeat of the land, our society would be more peaceful and attuned to our natural resources.

Having Time Away from the Clock and Commitments

Many teenagers live according the clock and according to what others tell them to do. At school it seems we have less control over our time than we will in any other part of our life. We're required by law to go to school from eight in the morning until three in the afternoon, then we're asked to go home and spend a number of hours on homework (at my school the average is three hours a night). Sports practices, play rehearsals, and band practice are just a few of the commitments that fill our time. We still live at home, so we're expected to attend family functions and help around the house. There just isn't much time left in the day once all those things are completed.

When I first started junior high school, my day was completely dictated by my watch. I timed my morning to the minute. I had 15 minutes in the bathroom to shower and brush my teeth, 15 minutes to get dressed and arrange my book bag for the day, and 15 minutes to prepare and eat breakfast. If for some reason I got ahead of schedule, I would use the remaining minutes to comb my hair or put a ribbon in it or something. I left the house at precisely 7:04 A.M. to catch the bus. I became so obsessed with time, my watch was a constant source of stress for me. I finally had to get rid of the watch in order to keep myself sane. Remarkably, I rarely missed the bus after relinquishing my watch.

Justin Monroe was also accustomed to his watch telling him where to be and when to be there. He didn't take his watch on solo. He realized that he was finally free from the confines of time that normally ruled his everyday life. He said it was a relief to take off his watch and not worry about the time. During his solo he said:

> Out of habit I still wanted to look at my watch because I thought that I should be doing something constructive or meaningful with my time, but as I watched a stream that ran by my campsite I found that for the first time in my life I truly was at peace in nature. I began to know the land. The frog pond behind my campsite became silent whenever an animal came toward the pond. I have since begun to really listen to what's around me.

Getting to Know Yourself Better

You spend many hours on solo just thinking. Besides the physical landscape around your site, there isn't much to think about except yourself. Solo is a time to question who you are and who you want to be. Through journal writing and intense thinking, teenagers often return from solo with a deeper understanding of self. This understanding comes from hours upon hours of just being with yourself. There isn't anyone or anything to distract you. Your only entertainment is yourself.

Ben became more deeply acquainted with himself through his awareness of intricacies in nature that he didn't usually notice in his normal life:

I sit here writing under my tarp with the patter of rain and the chirping of woodland creatures to set the ambiance. The air is crisp and cool and my bones are chilled. I bundle to stay warm and write with a fingerless glove. For the first time in a long time, I realize what I am: a human, an animal, a living organism. I am aware of my heartbeat and my breathing. I am aware that I am alive. I am aware that I will die. I have temporarily stopped and examined myself and what I am doing. I am existing and performing life functions. My body is constantly pumping out thoughts, criticism, anger and love and revelation. I am not merely Ben Pomeroy playing out some role or purpose. I am an organism fighting, creating, and loving in order to both survive and enjoy life.

Often this kind of self-knowledge can come from stream-of-consciousness journal writing. Writing whatever comes into my mind, without stopping to think, without lifting the pen from the page, and without stopping to worry about punctuation can allow for remarkable self-discovery.

Jessica tried this stream-of-consciousness technique in her journal, and felt she got to know herself much better:

I began to look back over what had been produced during the past 24 hours. [In my journal] I discovered that I had written over 30 pages. As I flipped back to a blank page to begin another marathon of words, something from the previous evening's writing caught my eye. I paused to read. As previously I had not been able to stop myself from writing, I now found that I could not stop myself from reading. I was caught up in the web of my own words, seeing them as if for the first time. I only vaguely remembered having written them. Certain individual words and phrases were distinctly mine. There were some thoughts I could conceive of having. But as a whole the writing was unfamiliar. As I read and reread the 30 pages, I found hidden within the trivial lists and mumbling an insight into myself that I had never experienced. This writing seemed more honest, less contrived, than any I had ever done, even in previous journal entries.

I found many things in that writing. I found that I had a capacity for personal expression I had never seen before. I found a bitterness over certain disadvantages in my life that I barely acknowledged as disadvantages. I found a passionate love for the squirrel that scurried along the stream, for the pines that lined the banks, and for the moss-covered rock that was my seat. I found secret desires I did not know existed. Clues to my inner self could be found in the connection I made between topics, in the particular words I chose, even in the varying size and legibility of my handwriting.

Frequently Asked Questions by Teenagers

Many of the general questions about Vision Quests are covered in Chapter 2. The questions below are often asked particularly by teenagers.

How can I do a solo?

The safest and easiest way to do a solo is to go with an organization that is trained in taking teenagers on solos. Some high schools have solo programs, as does Outward Bound. There are also many groups that take adults on Vision Quests that are slightly stricter than the teenage solos I have described, but many of them would welcome teenagers on their trips.

If it's not possible to go with an organization, you can plan your own trip. For safety, I strongly urge you to go with a group of friends. Get a group of about 3 to 10 friends together with at least one responsible adult, and choose an area where you probably won't run into many other people. For instance, I wouldn't do a solo in a park or any place in nature that is often frequented by tourists. Good locations are wilderness areas or national forests. Visit the area and pick your sites before you go out on solo. Make sure you can find them again.

Last spring (I was 17 years old at the time) I spent three weeks hiking with six friends in a primitive area in the canyons of Utah. We hired two adults, trained in taking teenagers into the wilderness, to come with us to ensure our safety. After we had hiked for two weeks, we prepared for a 24-hour solo. Our leaders scouted the area and found a suitable site for each of us. Mine was on a rock ledge above the canyon floor. I had a view up and down the length of the canyon. Periodically our leaders checked on us. If we needed anything or had any problems, we could signal them over to our site and ask for help. It was comforting knowing that they were there.

It's important that at least one responsible adult versed in outdoor survival goes with your group. Take the adults with you when you pick out your site so they know exactly where you are. They should set up a base camp and should be there at all times in case anyone in your group needs them. Every member should know the precise location of the base camp. When you go out on solo, the supervising adults should check on you at least twice a day. If you do not wish to see them, devise a system where you raise a flag in a designated spot each morning and each night, and they will lower it each time they come. If the flag is not raised, they will know that something may be wrong. You can also leave paper and pen at the flag for writing notes to the person checking on you. This is especially helpful if it rains and your clothes or sleeping bag get wet or if you need more water or food. You may also want to update them on your emotional well-being.

How do you pick your solo site?

When you pick your site, keep in mind that you should be near enough to your friends so that they can hear you if you shout or blow a whistle, but not so close that you can see one another. You should not break someone else's solo because you are bored, scared of things such as the dark or being alone, or if you can't stand the solitude. Though you may want to be far away from your friends, I can assure you that you will feel safer knowing you can reach them if necessary. *For your own safety, you must do your solo with friends nearby.*

If you're doing an extended solo of approximately four days, it's especially helpful to be near a lake or a stream. This way you will not need to carry in gallons of water. Take iodine pills or a water filter to treat all your water, as much of the water in the wilderness has bacteria that can make you quite sick. Properly treated water will be safe to drink. If you carry in your water, you need to bring plenty. You should drink approximately a gallon a day, though this varies for every person and the air temperature. Even though you'll not be doing anything physical on solo, it's still vital that you drink enough water.

Pick a site where you'll be comfortable for an extended period of time. For some this is high on a hill where you can look out at a view and feel uplifted, and for others it's being nestled within the trees. Be sure to find a flat place where you can sleep. A comfortable night's sleep will add to your overall enjoyment of your time alone in nature. The most important thing is to find somewhere in nature that makes you really happy.

How do you pack for a solo?

Pack appropriate clothes for the weather. Even if the forecast indicates pleasant weather while you are on solo, bring warm clothes. Weather can change in an instant. You won't be doing anything active, so it will take quite a bit more to keep your body warm. Take a closed-cell foam pad or an air mattress and a warm sleeping bag, preferably one you've used before so you know it will keep you warm. You may want to take a tarp and rope to build yourself a shelter in case of foul weather. You should definitely take a small first-aid kit, filled with bandages, antiseptic ointment, and a women's sanitary pad (this works remarkably well in absorbing blood if you get a deep cut). Though I haven't heard of anyone having any problems on a solo, it's always a good idea to be prepared.

Items you may also want to take: a journal and pen, a book, a flashlight, watercolors, a musical instrument, food, and toilet paper (carry this back out with you in a bag so you don't spoil the environment).

Can I take a book to read?

I have done solos with and without books. Many "hard-core" solo leaders would frown upon taking reading material because it removes you from your immediate surroundings. Although books can quite easily transport you away from the experience, certain books can help you better understand the land around you. On my solo in the canyons of Utah, I spent 24 hours perched high on a ledge looking down into the canyon below and up at the canyon walls above me. Anasazi ruins, pictographs, and petroglyphs decorated the canyon. On this solo I chose to read *Desert Solitaire* by Edward Abbey, and his descriptions of the canyon country gave me a deeper understanding of the area. My only suggestion in choosing a book is not to take any sort of reading that you *have* to do or *should* do. This would include books for school and college preparation guides. (I actually know a teenager who took college test vocabulary words with her to study.) Take a book that will inspire you spiritually or connect you more profoundly to the land.

Will I get better results if I fast?

No, not necessarily. Some teenagers choose to fast on solo, following the traditional way of Native Americans. Others choose to take food. The Native Americans fasted so the spirits would take pity on them and come to them in a vision. I believe both ways lead to results. I have done the majority of my solos with food. If I don't have it with me, I become infatuated with it. It's all I can think about. Most teenagers are still growing, so I think it's important to take food. The solo I had just completed in Utah was the first time I didn't have anything to eat. I would like to say that that solo was more powerful because I fasted, but I honestly didn't notice any difference in the results.

The traditional reason to go without food is to cleanse your body and to keep you from getting too caught up in the preparing and eating of the food. If you think you want to do a solo without food, I suggest taking it with you with the intention of not eating it. I have a friend who took all the food with him that the Mountain School told him to take, but he didn't eat any of it. Christina Capone also took all the prescribed food with her, but with the intention of eating it. On her solo she found that she wasn't very hungry. She returned from the woods after her four-day solo with her food bag full, having eaten only her chocolate bars and apples.

Everyone's body is different, and only you know if you can fast on solo comfortably. If you choose to fast on a lengthy solo, I suggest doing a practice run in the comfort of your own home. Try fasting from morning until evening and see how you feel. If you have any question about your comfort, take some food with you. You do not have to eat it. Most important, remember that you do not need to be an ascetic to attain results.

How far should I be from other people?

If you do a solo with an organization or a group, they will place you a certain distance apart from others. In most cases, this is at least a hundred yards apart or within hearing distance of a whistle, but out of sight of one another. If you're creating your own quest, before the solo begins, sit in your circle and yell to make sure that the others can hear you.

What if someone does comes near my site and starts talking to me?

The best thing to do if this happens is to explain what you are doing. The person most likely will respect your desire for privacy and will leave you alone.

Should I take a journal?

Journal writing can be a great way to unleash the thoughts and feelings in your head and leave you with a lasting memento of your solo, though, like a book, journal writing can distance you from your surroundings. When writing, you can become oblivious to the weather and the landscape. There's also a tendency to analyze too much and to think too much. In a solo entry of mine, I wrote vigorously for a number of pages, then I ended the entry by saying: "I feel like I'm analyzing this experience far too much already, and it's only the first hour or so."

In her journal, Jessica released feelings through vigorous writing:

I awoke at dawn, momentarily perplexed by my surroundings. After pausing for a few moments to get reacquainted with my forest home, [I thought I would write] until I was completely calm. . . . The words just continued to flow. It seemed that I could not stop myself; I wrote without effort, without pausing to think. For the next two days, I continued to write to fend off lingering fears, loneliness, and tears. Putting a continuous stream of words on paper made me calm during those four days, and has ever since. Those words allowed me to look into my soul, to see the person that existed away from society and its constraints. Via words, I survived solo and gained insight into who I am.

Is it okay to walk around my solo site?

It's okay to walk around a bit. You will certainly need to walk to the stream or lake if you don't bring water with you. You will also want to be far from your site when defecating; however, I would suggest not exploring too far from your site. The main reason for this is safety, but also staying in one place encourages careful examination of your immediate surroundings and a sharp focus on your thoughts without distractions.

What is a good age to go on my first solo?

The age that a child does the first solo completely depends on the individual. I don't believe I could have handled a lengthy solo before age 13. The majority of teenagers I know who have done solos are about 16 or 17, which is a good age because you're old enough to deal with the fear and the boredom, but still shaping and defining who you want to be. This time alone is a great way to focus on yourself and identify the parts of your character that you want to accentuate in your future.

Younger children can do an abridged version of solo by sitting in a garden for a few hours alone. I know a mother who created a sacred circle in her backyard for her ten-year-old daughter to do a four-hour solo. The mother stayed nearby to make sure the experience was enjoyable for her child, and the young girl was completely ecstatic afterward. I believe that you can get just as many results from a short solo as from a long solo. Your intention is much more important than the time that you spend. One time I sat in a hayfield for an hour, wrote in my journal, and gained as much of a clear sense of my direction as I got from the four-day solo. (However, it's fair to say that the time spent on my solos and Quests may have prepared me for that special hour.)

Is it okay to bring materials to remember the location, such as a camera, paints, pens, and so forth?

Solo is a time to live with the bare necessities, to live deliberately, so it's best to leave all modern devices at home. However, I think paints are a great way to study the landscape and have something to remember it by when you return to your normal life. I don't suggest taking a camera, though. If I have my camera with me I have difficulty immersing myself in nature. Rather, I see nature in terms of photography textures, patterns, shapes, and shades of gray. The stream, the rain, the woodland creatures all become subjects, and I forget that I can learn about myself from these things. If you really want a photograph of your solo site, take a camera with you when you first go out to scout for your site before you actually go out on solo.

What if I get lonely, bored, or scared?

You may encounter all three of these things, but that is all part of the experience. You will grow from pushing through the loneliness, moving to the state beyond boredom, and facing your fears. If the loneliness, the boredom, or the fear gets to be too much, or if you just aren't enjoying yourself, you have the right at any time to break your solo. It's not a sign of weakness or lack of courage to break solo. You can do it at any time. If you do go with a group of other teenagers, please remember that you cannot break anyone else's solo. No matter how bored you get, you cannot enter someone else's site and disturb their solitude.

What if my solo doesn't feel enlightening or life changing?

Solo can be many things for different people. Sometimes solo experiences will allow you to realize things about yourself and make decisions that will entirely change your life. But solo isn't always an incredible experience. Often, solo can be just a pleasant and restful way to spend a few days. When going into a solo, it's best not to think that this is the one and only time that you'll do this—that puts unnecessary pressure on you for it to be an amazing experience. You can do as many solos in your lifetime as you wish. They will each be different.

Can a solo help me with a problem or life direction?

If you go into a solo with the intention of answering a question or solving a problem, you may find some answers. Sometimes you have to search for answers and wait for signs, and other times they come to you "clear as day."

When I was on my four-day solo in New Hampshire I spent a great deal of time thinking. I went on that solo without my journal, a book, or paints. I spent 72 hours sitting beside my make-shift tarp shelter, beneath the canopy of hardwood trees, just thinking. I thought about a great many things in those 72 hours. One of the main things that kept coming to my mind was love. I thought about my friends who had boyfriends and wondered when it would be my turn. In the few weeks prior to solo, many couples had started to form around school. I sat in my solo site and counted 6 new couples out of the 45 students in the school. I couldn't figure it out. Why had love never happened to me? I was 17 and tired of waiting. I stared at a small shrub with a solitary dead leaf hanging from its branches. I asked nature to give me a sign whether love was in my near future. If the answer was yes, I expected this leaf to fall from the branch. I thought this was a good setup because it was sure to fall soon anyway. Just as I made this deal with the power of nature, I heard a raucous noise behind me. I turned my head to see what was happening. There were two squirrels mating in the tree behind me, chasing each other up and down the trunk and across the branches. I thought this was a good sign.

Someone once asked me why I have been on so many solos. I told him that I love having the time to be by myself in nature to think and to just to "be," without the constraints of time. A solo gives me a sense of peace, a chance to know myself a little better and to feel independent from others. The values I've learned and the knowledge I've gained on solo have been invaluable. I can take what I have learned on solo and apply it to the rest of my life. I wish all teenagers could have this opportunity.

CHAPTER SEVEN

INTEGRATING YOUR QUEST INTO YOUR LIFE

There's usually an adjustment period after any kind of Quest, whether it's an extended retreat in nature or a pilgrimage or a Vision Walk. It's important to comprehend some of the transitions that may occur as you incorporate your vision into your life. It's also useful to understand some of the potential pitfalls and how to avoid them so that your integration period is easy and joyous.

The most usual comment I receive from people in the months and years after a Quest is that they feel a much deeper communion with loved ones, and often they also experience a depth of universal love for all beings. Rick Maurico, a lighting technician from Great Britian, shared these sentiments with me about how his relationships changed as a result of his Quest:

> *It's been almost three years since my Vision Quest. As a result of my Quest I find that I have deeper relations with everyone I meet, and I know they feel the same. There's a "connectedness" that pervades every encounter. I find that even when I pass people on the street, particularly children, they often change from being angry to gleeful. They seem to mirror what they feel from me, which is generally joy.*
>
> *I've discovered that being myself is my truth. I've found the Me that was always there, and I've understood some of the reasons behind who I am. One of the most profound realizations I've had is that is that being who I am is enough.*
>
> *Personal relationships have also changed for me in a positive way. I now understand the many aspects of love . . . and I understand that giving and receiving are much the same thing.*

I understand the camaraderie felt by men for men that goes beyond words or actions. Souls touching souls. I also know that a woman, who is one's partner, must feel that she is special, even while the man [whom she is with] is feeling unconditional love for everyone and everything. I know this seems a simple thing to understand but I have been incredibly slow in matters of the heart.

After a Vision Quest or a pilgrimage, the world is the same, and yet very different. For most, life no longer seems random and arbitrary. Seemingly unrelated events begin to take on meaning and offer signs and personal messages. The messages were always there but now one becomes aware of them and the desire to follow them can become very strong. This is fine if the changes that are made are in harmony with conventional life. However, the challenge comes when society, friends, and family feel that you're supposed to embark on a certain path of action, even though your vision points you in another direction.

When you begin to grow spiritually, sometimes the people who are closest to you are threatened by that change. Part of their definition of Self depends on the relationship patterns that have developed between you and them. When you change, it can potentially threaten the personality dynamics of everyone who is close to you because they may feel that they have to change as well. However, although there's an adjustment period after returning from a Vision Quest, usually after a settling in period others see the power and beauty of the change and everyone benefits. A spouse or child or parent of a Quester will often come to my Vision Quest the following year because of the improvement they have perceived in their loved one.

One participant's husband did a Quest after she returned from her Quest.

Shortly after I returned from my Vision Quest in the United States, my husband decided to take off to the mountains just north of Cape Town to do a four-day Vision Quest. Upon his return home, I was mesmerized by the life and passion in his eyes. I know what you must see, Denise, when we all return from our circles! It's been easy and natural talking to him, now, about all aspects of this side of my life.

Another participant wrote about the transition that she experienced on her return:

I came back home, unable to give words to what I had experienced. I felt free and I felt a need to protect that freedom. Fitting into the rhythm of my family environment posed a new challenge. My husband and I could not connect. Yet my whole being cried out for connection. The yin and yang parts of myself had some hard work to find wholeness. The Vision Quest was truly a search for my own identity and reevaluating my life. It was a big adventure and it put me back feeling in control of my life. Now I feel more control over the choices I make.

This participant and her husband were able to overcome, in a positive way, the temporary distance they experienced after her return from the Quest, but their experience was not uncommon. Be aware that some people in your life may feel unsettled if you are changed by your experience.

Another Quest participant had consistently taken the role of a helper/caretaker for everyone in her life. After the Quest she felt a surge of empowerment and self-assertiveness fill her and she decided to make some changes in her life. This challenged others who had entered into the victim/savior dynamic with her. She said that some friends were upset with her: "What do you mean you're not going to be in charge of the car pool anymore?" "What do you mean you're not going to watch my kids every Friday night?" However, she said that extraordinary strength came from finding her truth and listening to her inner voice. It took a few months for friends to adjust to the "new" person. Although a few friends fell away, this participant reported that she felt a much deeper connection to people because her friendships were based on mutual respect rather than on need.

Even if you don't have the support of other people, there's power in following the guidance that occurs during your Quest. If you are concerned about the changes that a Quest might bring into your relationships, ask yourself: *Do I want to live a life fulfilling the expectations of other people, or do I want to be an individual who is willing to make a stand in life? Do I want to be a person who lives their truth? Do I want to be a person who says, "This is what I believe. This is who I am. This is my path"?* If you are, then the changes that occur in your relationships will be for the good of all.

A Quest can change the way you view the world. There are two ways of looking at the world. One is the ordinary way that people born into Western culture have come to accept. Ordinary reality dictates that objects and events in life, though they may seem to influence one another, are nevertheless separate. A second way of observing the world is that there's a sacred pattern of energy that underlies all life and that, in the most profound sense, we're not separate from the world around us.

In Western culture we're trained from early childhood to embrace the first way of being, even though in school sports, for example, we're taught about team spirit and working together. However, a deeper perception reveals an energy of competitiveness that underlies our entire educational system. Believing in a random and separate world has survival value. In desperate times, isolation, competitiveness, and separation perhaps can keep one alive. After a Quest, however, a belief in a flowing universe often evolves, where every act has consequences on the world at large. This brings a quality of mystery and insight that greatly enriches life but can at the same time bring concern and puzzlement from friends and family: "What do you mean that the wind told you to quit your job. Are you crazy?"

One participant wrote about how the shift of perception of reality affected his life:

*For me the Vision Quest offered a significant shift in how
I perceive reality. Before the Quest I perceived reality much the
same as a photograph of a moment in time. Now reality seems*

more like a hologram of the same. I'm able to allow other per-spectives to be experienced as my life unfolds. My Vision Quest has been a joyous journey, opening my heart and mind to the beautiful depths of feelings. It truly empowers me to be of ser-vice to others in this life.

After a Quest, individuals often report changes in their decision-making process. They report feeling a greater sense of certainty once they have made a decision, and they find that the amount of time needed to make a decision is shorter.

In the usual course of life, to make a decision we embark on a logical course of investigation. We gather and compare the facts and then, through a process of elimination and analysis, come to a conclusion. However, there's another way to make decisions. During your Quest, when you begin to step into that quiet inner place of wisdom and clarity, it sets in motion a new way of making decisions. Instead of the linear process, you may find that you "just know" the right choice. Sometimes there won't be any concrete data to prove your decision, but there's a gut response inside you that says: "This just feels right." In my experience, decisions made in this fashion are much more satisfying, for they have emerged through intuition and instinct. It's valuable to gather and analyze data for any life-affecting decision, but making a decision solely on logic and rational reasoning often yields less beneficial results than a choice made, after amassing information, from intuition. As R.M. said:

There's often but a moment to make a choice, and in the past I usually let the moment pass and later regretted for a long time my decisions reached through inaction. Now I find that I am able to make decisions much more easily and effortlessly.

Another Quest participant, M.J., said:

Yes, something happened to me on Sacred Island. I don't know if it's so important to analyze what happened because I have lived my whole life analyzing everything. After the Vision

Quest I decided to give up analyzing so much and to give room for more miracles in my life.

Problems don't necessarily disappear after your Quest, but often you experience a shift in the way you view them. Instead of problems being seen as insurmountable difficulties, they become challenges; personal obstacles are seen in the context of growth and spiritual development.

Before Joseph came to the Vision Quest, he had had a boundary dispute for 11 years with his next-door neighbor. During those years his neighbor could be downright nasty to Joseph and his wife, making neighborhood life sometimes intolerable. After the Quest, Joseph went out to this garden, looked over the fence, and saw his neighbor in his garden. It was the first time in almost 11 years that Joseph didn't feel a tightness in the pit of his stomach when he saw him. He surprised himself by saying "Hi!" to his neighbor. The neighbor was just as surprised as Joseph was by this friendly gesture. Although the border dispute didn't go away, it bothered Joseph less and less. He said that after the Quest he began to see all the value that he had gained over the 11 years of disagreement, and it completely altered the way he viewed his relationship with his neighbor.

Sometimes life is like a still pool that looks clear for the top few inches, but beneath the clear water lies a deep reservoir of silt and algae. If a fresh, crystal clear stream flows into the stagnant pool, it stirs up the pool so it looks murky. Eventually, however, the pool becomes clear to the golden sandy bottom. This can parallel what can occur during and after a Quest. Sometimes, before the Quest, life may seem calm and serene, but beneath the surface are a number of unresolved issues. The Vision Quest is like the clear water flowing into a stagnant pool, stirring up old issues. So it may seem that after the Quest there's a surfeit of problems. These difficulties may be uncomfortable, but it's healthy to deal with them; eventually they will vanish from your life.

Going on a Vision Quest doesn't necessarily mean that you won't have any problems afterward. But what often occurs is that your ability to deal with problems becomes quicker, so that you don't hold on to them for so long. Even though most people think they don't want problems, problems aren't really the dilemma: It's *attachment* to problems that creates difficulty. For example, if everyone's problems were thrown into a circle and you could choose any, wouldn't you be quick to retrieve your own? Part of the experience of living on this planet is having problems, and your ability to detach from them can free up life-force energy so that you become more vital and exuberant.

It's not uncommon for one's definition of self to alter after a Quest. Often our sense of self comes from definitions that others have given us about who we are. When you take time to be quiet and sit in nature, the boundaries of self expand beyond the body. The limitations imposed by others and society begin to lift, and you see yourself in a new light. Wild Flower, a New Zealand international flight attendant, said:

> *During the Quest I felt layers of my inner being were being peeled away like an onion. As one layer was exposed and cleaned, there would be another. I worked through deep childhood traumas that I had never been aware were affecting me, leading me to a peace and connectedness that I had never felt before. Looking back, the difference I feel is that of a parachute full of old stuff being dragged around behind me being released, leaving me feeling much lighter, almost floating.*

People often report that before the Quest, self-esteem comes from what they do; afterward, it begins to come from who they are. Mervi, the podiatrist from Finland, said:

> *When I decided to go to the Vision Quest I really didn't have any good reasons for traveling to the other side of the world. Maybe I had to get far enough away from my normal environment and go to a safe place where I couldn't run away from myself and my life anymore. Before the Quest I was a doer. I gained acceptance in life through what I did. Also I had difficulties with my emotions. I never met a person who I trusted*

enough to tell about my feelings. I felt that I was covered by thick ice. Living was like driving a car with ten safety belts on. Life was a "slow" depression that caused different pains to my body. As a result of the Quest I have learned to feel more, and this has been the beginning of my new life. I still have problems with things like letting go. But now I have insight about it, and I believe that I can learn more. I am at the beginning and I won't stop.

In normal life we usually identify ourselves in the context of our family, which is usually defined as relatives and close friends. Often after a Quest the sense of self expands beyond ordinary parameters to include a greater circle of relationships and family. According to Lin B., a British professional reflexologist:

I left the Vision Quest with such happiness and confidence, something I have always been lacking. The whole concept of family now has a different meaning. Family is now, to me, everything in the universe.

I have been particularly encouraged to see the vast array of newly discovered talents and abilities that emerge for so many after a Quest. Lin B. also mentioned that she is now able to see her previously undiscovered abilities:

As I looked back on my life I realized I always had the strength to get through difficult situations and was able to see the healing power that I always had. I now have the courage to help people with this same power.

The power of the Quest is to allow you to understand the deep current of intent that propels your life while at the same time allowing you to recognize that you are doing exactly what you should be doing in life. Every experience has brought you to where you are now; and where you are now is at a pinnacle in your evolution. Quests, no matter what form they take, contribute to the understanding that there are no accidents in life. Even mundane aspects of life are propelling you on your spiritual path. Even those things that you judged in yourself or in others are "on purpose." Every experience you have allows you to become brighter, lighter, and closer to the Creator. There's a divine plan for your life and everything that happens to you is a part of that plan. This can bring a deep sense of relief, for many people feel a longing for purpose in life. *Even if you don't leave a Quest knowing exactly what your purpose is, you are nevertheless fulfilling your purpose perfectly. You always have been.*

It's not uncommon after a Quest to have a deeper sense of patience for self and others. Impatience and lack of acceptance usually have at their root a lack of self-esteem. For as self-esteem grows during a Quest, acceptance of life circumstances grows. The impatient desire to achieve more and faster is often replaced with a calmer motivation, which usually produces greater results with less effort. Susan, a systems analyst from Chicago, said:

> *In the four years since my Quest, I feel much more satisfied with what I have and who I am. This doesn't mean that I don't have goals. I do have goals and things I want to attain in my life. I used to feel that if I wasn't constantly achieving, I wasn't a worthwhile person. However, now I strive for goals because it's fun, rather than feeling a compulsion to be a high achiever.*

Lennart is a very respected, high-level Swedish businessman. He wrote to me describing how he felt he gained more patience and acceptance after his Quest on Sacred Island:

> *I am really much more happy with my life after the Vision Quest. In my daily life, now there have been not only one, but many occasions when I have been surprised about the way I have managed to handle things. My employees have mentioned more than once that they now have a leader and coach who has high human values. I realized very strongly during the Vision Quest course that I often judged people. I wanted them to behave like me, for example, to be on time for the class, and not ask silly questions, and so forth. I noticed your patience; how you accepted people, even if they were late, and how you answered every*

question, and even if it was quite clear that the person who asked the question just wanted to hear her/his own voice. I had an instantaneous shift, which I experienced during the course.

Another very noticeable shift, which has occurred and grown stronger each day, is that I have stopped trying so hard to achieve my goals. I have become much more subtle [relaxed] in my approach to daily tasks and I dare say that I am more successful that way. When I look back on my life and think about how many times I have failed because of trying too hard, it's a relief finally to become "enlightened" and realize that "it's not good, it's not bad, we've not seen the whole story yet." My stress level is lower, not because I have less to do in my work, but because something has changed in me and I now see things differently.

I am more content with my life. At the Quest I was looking for guidance about how I should continue my life. I was very uncomfortable and unsure about my daily life. However, during my time on the island, I realized that I am on the right path. There's a purpose in my present job, and as soon as I have completed that purpose I will be able to continue. This I have felt strongly [since the Quest]. I also daresay that I enjoy the present moment in a completely new way.

Lennart also realized that the focus of his Quest wasn't to overcome fears, it was to learn to live at peace in the present:

Quite early I realized that the Quest wasn't for me to meet my fears but more to understand that this is it. . . . I live here and now. This has made me feel much more secure in my life. [Because I am a man who is always busy] it was a relief when, during the second day [of my Quest], I realized that I was content and felt inspiration flow through my body . . . without doing anything. For me, with all my demands always to do something, this was a relief. This is probably the most important thing I learned during the Vision Quest. I have definitely incorporated this into the way I live and work today, and I don't feel frustrated when I don't manage to fulfill all my plans. I know there's a new day tomorrow.

It's difficult to live fully if you are afraid of dying. Fear of death can be a sinister subconscious undercurrent in your life. When you begin to see yourself and your life in a large context during your Quest, there emerges a sense of self that is beyond the body. You realize that you inhabit a body but are not your body. You are Spirit, infinite and everlasting. When this relationship occurs, fear of death begins to drop away and a deep relaxation fills its place.

One participant spoke about how her Quest changed her perception of death:

> Many things have changed since the Quest. For example, I'm not afraid of death anymore. In addition, different fears have begun to drop away. For example, the first time that I ever really enjoyed flying was my journey from Seattle to New York [after the Quest]. It was wonderful! I was sitting on the plane, drum in my arms, having fun. The whole experience on the island was the best time of my life!

Suggestions for After Your Vision Quest

Be understanding of the responses of others to your Quest. It's important when you return home after a Quest to be sensitive to others' responses. You may feel like a hero returning from a great odyssey, but instead of a hero's welcome, you are met with indifference, disbelief, envy, or even hostility. Be compassionate, as it can be difficult for others to understand what you have been through unless they have been through a similar experience. Once, immediately following a very intensive inner Quest in Europe, I went to visit a friend who had a large house in London. I arrived at her home feeling such overwhelming compassion and love for all living beings that when the housekeeper opened the door, I embraced him and told him I loved him. Though secretly I'm sure he was pleased, on the surface he was quite startled by my unexpected sentiments. This experience deepened my realization that it's not only valuable to take time to become grounded after a Quest, it's also important to be understanding of the responses of others.

Sometimes there's an advantage in not talking at length about your experience in the weeks and months afterward. It's a seed within you that has been planted in your deep subconscious that will sprout and bear fruit in the years to come. And like all seeds in their initial stages of growth, it needs to be protected. Those who want to know will seek you out. Sometimes talking too much about your experience to those who don't understand can diminish the sacredness of your vision, so be discriminating about what you say and to whom you say it.

Be wary of high expectations. High expectations can sometimes cause difficulty after a Quest. Tony's marriage was falling apart and he thought that if he did a Quest it would help keep his marriage together. He was disappointed to find after his Quest that his wife still wanted to leave him. However, he reported that his Quest had helped him deal with the separation in a more harmonious way. Sometimes high expectations come from family and friends who desire dramatic changes in their loved one; this occurs especially with teenage Questers. A Quest is very individual. Sometimes people have immediate and dramatic results. Sometimes the results from a Quest are deep and internal, without exterior results for months or years. Honor the process in whatever form it takes.

Don't make sudden changes. Sometimes immediately after a Quest there's such a sense of exhilaration and freedom that there's a tendency to want to throw off the fetters of society and make immediate and dramatic changes in life. This course of action has served some people who otherwise might have become bogged down in old patterns and habits; however, for most people, I suggest letting some time go by while your vision becomes integrated into your everyday life. Don't make any dramatic changes until you have had some time to assess their implications in your life.

Integrating Your Vision into Your Life

When you return to ordinary life, the dishes and the laundry still need to be done and bills need to be paid. In Zen Buddhism there's a maxim: "Before enlightenment, chop wood and carry water . . . after enlightenment, chop wood and carry water." The Quest is not about turning away from ordinary life but rather embracing it with compassion, integrity, and joy. Though the outward form of life may remain the same, your inner life begins to change. It's as if an ember of spirit in the soul has been fanned by the winds of heaven to become an inner flame that will burn deeply and brightly throughout your life.

A Quest done with intent and an open heart is like a pebble dropped in a still pool; the ripples will touch the furthest shores of your consciousness. Even in those times after a Quest, when the vision seems so far away—"Was it all a dream? Did it really happen?"—the inner flame continues to burn. Your vision will grow inside you. Even in the darkest moments. Even when you're unsure of yourself. Even when you're angry or afraid. This is the power of the vision.

May your Quest be the beginning of an adventure that leads you to the center of your soul.

ENDNOTES

Chapter 1

1. John (Fire) Lame Deer and Richard Erdoes, *Lame Deer, Seeker of Visions* (New York: Pocket Books, 1976) [London: Davis-Poynter, 1973].

Chapter 2

1. Joseph Campbell, *The Hero with a Thousand Faces* (Princeton, NJ: Princeton University Press, 1970) [London: Grafton Books, 1988].

2. For more information, see Denise Linn, *Sacred Space: Clearing and Enhancing the Energy of Your Home* (New York: Ballantine Books, 1995) and *Space Clearing A–Z* (Carlsbad, CA: Hay House, Inc.).
    For further study of signs, see Denise Linn, *The Secret Language of Signs* (New York: Ballantine Books, 1976).

Chapter 3

1. Mai-mai Sze, *The Way of Chinese Painting* (New York: Random House, 1959).

Chapter 5

1. Joseph Epes Brown, *The Sacred Pipe: Black Elk's Account of the Seven Rites of the Oglala Sioux* (Norman: University of Oklahoma Press, 1953).

FURTHER INFORMATION

For additional information about Quests, visit **DeniseLinn .com** or contact spiritual teacher Catriona MacGregor.

Catriona (Gaelic for Catherine), who has trained with Denise, helps people find greater meaning in their own lives, through Vision Quests, Nature Quests, and Spirit Quests. Since childhood, Catriona has had mystical experiences in nature that have provided her with a profound understanding of the world. Her Quests are held at beautiful, inspiring places in Northern California, as well as in Scotland and New Zealand.

Catriona is the author of *Partnering with Nature: The Wild Path to Reconnecting with the Earth,* the winner of a gold medal from the Nautilus Book Awards, which recognizes world-changing books that promote spiritual growth and social change. She is also a contributing author of *Healing the Heart of the World: Harnessing the Power of Intention to Change Your Life and the Planet,* along with Caroline Myss, Masaru Emoto, Thich Nhat Hanh, and others. To learn more about Catriona's Vision Quests, go to **www .naturalpathfinder.com**.

Denise suggests that to prepare for a Quest, you might consider going on a 28-day inner and outer program as outlined in her book *Soul Coaching®: 28 Days to Discover Your Authentic Self.* To find a professional certified Soul Coach to assist you in this preparation journey, visit Denise's website. Some of the Soul Coaches also lead Quests after the 28-day program.

ACKNOWLEDGMENTS

I am deeply grateful to my Cherokee ancestors for the guidance they have given me during my Quests. Additionally, I'm profoundly thankful to the people who participated in my Quests over the years. They have inspired me and showed me new ways of teaching.

I also thank the individuals who have worked with me to make my Quests a success over the years, especially Lynette Orman and Ellie Baker. These remarkable women brought wisdom and grace to each Vision Quest. Also much gratitude to Patti Hanmer, William Daniel-Braham, and Pauline Howfield.

I'm immensely grateful to my remarkable editor at Random House, Judith Kendra; to my sister, Heather Fortner; and to Mervi Jakonen. Additional gratitude to the wonderful Lisa Mitchell and Shannon Littrell at Hay House, and to Carol Barnette and Kathy Dannel Vitcak for helping bring this book to fruition.

I especially thank my husband, David, for his continued kindness and compassion. And a very special thank-you to our daughter, Meadow, who truly inspired the creation of this book.

— D.L.

A heartfelt thanks to my parents. To my mom, who took me on my first Quest at age 13 and gave me the opportunity to write about teenage solos; and to my dad, who read my drafts and always told me they were good, no matter how much work they still needed, I'm thankful.

Acknowledgments

I'd also like to thank:

Everyone at the Mountain School for the best experience of my life. I especially thank the director, Anne Stephens, and the teachers who spent many weeks preparing me for my lengthy solo.

Christina Capone, Abigail Chatfield, Allison Cohen, Sarah Levin, Justin Monroe, Ben Pomeroy, Jessica Taverna, and Gwyn Welles, who sent me descriptions of their solo experiences.

The Lakeside Wilderness Program, which first took me into the backcountry.

And finally, a heartfelt thank-you to the Maine Coast Semester, where I taught high-school students for three years and ran their solo program, calling upon my own teenage Quest experiences.

— M.L.

ABOUT THE AUTHORS

Denise Linn's personal journey began as a result of a near-death experience at age 17. Her life-changing experiences and remarkable recovery set her on a spiritual quest that led her to explore the healing traditions of many cultures, including those of her own Cherokee ancestors, the Aborigines in the Australian bush, and the Zulus in Bophuthatswana. She trained with a Hawaiian kahuna (shaman), and Reiki Master Hawayo Takata. She was also adopted into a New Zealand Maori tribe. In addition, Denise lived in a Zen Buddhist monastery for more than two years.

Denise is an internationally renowned teacher in the field of self-development. She's the author of the bestseller *Sacred Space* and the award-winning *Feng Shui for the Soul*, and has written 16 books, which are available in 24 languages. Denise has appeared in numerous documentaries and television shows worldwide, gives seminars on six continents and is the founder of the International Institute of Soul Coaching®, which offers professional certification programmes in life coaching.

For information about Denise's certification programme and other lectures, please visit her website or write to: Denise Linn Seminars, P.O. Box 759, Paso Robles, California 93447, USA.

www.deniselinn.com
www.facebook.com/DeniseLinn.author

ABOUT THE AUTHORS

Meadow Linn co-wrote this book and also wrote Chapter 6 based on her experiences as a teenager on Quests. She received her bachelor's degree from Williams College and her master's degree from Columbia University, and is the co-author of *The Mystic Cookbook.* Meadow writes a food and lifestyle column for a Seattle newspaper.

www.savortheday.com

NOTES

NOTES

NOTES

NOTES

NOTES

NOTES

NOTES

NOTES

NOTES

NOTES

Hay House Titles of Related Interest

YOU CAN HEAL YOUR LIFE, the movie, starring Louise L. Hay & Friends
(available as a 1-DVD program and an expanded 2-DVD set)
Watch the trailer at: **www.LouiseHayMovie.com**

THE SHIFT, the movie,
starring Dr Wayne W. Dyer
(available as a 1-DVD program and an expanded 2-DVD set)
Watch the trailer at: **www.DyerMovie.com**

∾

ASK YOUR GUIDES: How to Contact your Angels and Spirit Helpers,
by Sonia Choquette

FLOWER THERAPY: Welcome the Angels of Nature into Your Life,
by Doreen Virtue and Robert Reeves

HEART THOUGHTS: A Treasury of Inner Wisdom, by Louise L. Hay

*MESSAGES FROM SPIRIT: The Extraordinary Power of Oracles,
Omens, and Signs,* by Colette Baron-Reid

101 WAYS TO JUMP-START YOUR INTUITION, by John Holland

WISHES FULFILLED: Mastering the Art of Manifesting,
by Dr Wayne W. Dyer

All of the above are available at your local bookstore,
or may be ordered by contacting Hay House (see next page).

∾

We hope you enjoyed this Hay House book. If you'd like to receive our online catalogue featuring additional information on Hay House books and products, or if you'd like to find out more about the Hay Foundation, please contact:

Hay House UK, Ltd, 292B Kensal Rd., London W10 5BE
Phone: 0-20-8962-1230 • Fax: 0-20-8962-1239
www.hayhouse.co.uk • www.hayfoundation.org

∾

Published and distributed in Australia by: Hay House Australia Pty. Ltd., 18/36 Ralph St., Alexandria NSW 2015 • *Phone:* 612-9669-4299 *Fax:* 612-9669-4144 • www.hayhouse.com.au

Published and distributed in the United States by: Hay House, Inc., P.O. Box 5100, Carlsbad, CA 92018-5100 • Phone: (1) 760 431-7695 or (1) 800 654-5126 • Fax: (1) 760 431-6948 or (1) 800 650-5115 www.hayhouse.com®

Published and distributed in the Republic of South Africa by: Hay House SA (Pty), Ltd., P.O. Box 990, Witkoppen 2068 *Phone/Fax:* 27-11-467-8904 • www.hayhouse.co.za

Published in India by: Hay House Publishers India, Muskaan Complex, Plot No. 3, B-2, Vasant Kunj, New Delhi 110 070 • *Phone:* 91-11-4176-1620 • *Fax:* 91-11-4176-1630 • www.hayhouse.co.in

Distributed in Canada by: Raincoast, 9050 Shaughnessy St., Vancouver, B.C. V6P 6E5 • *Phone:* (604) 323-7100 • *Fax:* (604) 323-2600 • www.raincoast.com

∾

Take Your Soul on a Vacation

Visit **www.HealYourLife.com®** to regroup, recharge, and reconnect with your own magnificence. Featuring blogs, mind-body-spirit news, and life-changing wisdom from Louise Hay and friends.

Visit **www.HealYourLife.com** today!

JOIN THE HAY HOUSE FAMILY

As the leading self-help, mind, body and spirit publisher in the UK, we'd like to welcome you to our family so that you can enjoy all the benefits our website has to offer.

 EXTRACTS from a selection of your favourite author titles

 COMPETITIONS, PRIZES & SPECIAL OFFERS Win extracts, money off, downloads and so much more

 LISTEN to a range of radio interviews and our latest audio publications

 CELEBRATE YOUR BIRTHDAY An inspiring gift will be sent your way

 LATEST NEWS Keep up with the latest news from and about our authors

 ATTEND OUR AUTHOR EVENTS Be the first to hear about our author events

 iPHONE APPS Download your favourite app for your iPhone

 HAY HOUSE INFORMATION Ask us anything, all enquiries answered

join us online at **www.hayhouse.co.uk**

 292B Kensal Road, London W10 5BE
T: 020 8962 1230 E: info@hayhouse.co.uk